THE SPIRIT AND THE DRUM

THE SPIRIT AND THE DRUM

A MEMOIR OF AFRICA

EDITH TURNER

THE UNIVERSITY OF ARIZONA PRESS

TUCSON

ABOUT THE AUTHOR

EDITH TURNER is a British-born anthropologist, and the widow of anthropologist Victor Turner. She teaches at the University of Virginia. *The Spirit and the Drum* grew out of fieldwork in Central Africa from 1951 to 1954, in 1966, and in 1985. Because of her unpressurized relationship with the Ndembu women she lived among, she was able to gather material on such sensitive matters as sexuality and the meaning of initiation. This book, then, became one about her personal adventures; it turned out to be more poetic than technical because poetry is her real love.

The lines from "The Ninth Elegy" from *Duino Elegies* by Rainer Maria Rilke, translated by J. B. Leishman and Stephen Spender, are reprinted by permission of W. W. Norton & Company, Inc. Copyright 1939 by W. W. Norton & Company, Inc. Copyright renewed 1967 by Stephen Spender and J. B. Leishman.

Frontispiece: Edith Turner in Kajima.

THE UNIVERSITY OF ARIZONA PRESS
Copyright © 1987
The Arizona Board of Regents
All Rights Reserved

This book was set in Palatino
Manufactured in the U.S.A.

LIBRARY OF CONGRESS CATALOGING IN PUBLICATION DATA

Turner, Edith L. B., 1921–
    The spirit and the drum.

    Includes index.
      1. Ndembu (African people)—Rites and ceremonies.
    2. Ndembu (African people)—Social life and customs.
    3. Turner, Edith L. B., 1921– . 4. Ethnology—
    Field work.   I. Title.
    DT963.42.T77   1987   306'.089963   86-30825
    ISBN 0-8165-1009-1 (alk. paper)

British Library Cataloguing in Publication data are available.

Dedicated to the Loving Memory of
Victor Turner
1920–1983

CONTENTS

PREFACE

WHEN ANTHROPOLOGISTS WRITE BOOKS, their style is clear and dispassionate, for the presentation of information and its analysis is primary. Their objectivity makes possible the accumulation of concrete knowledge, and by means of well-attested methods enlarges our understanding of the social environment of humans in many cultures. In this book I am doing something different. I aim to recreate as experience the cultural events Victor Turner and I witnessed among the Ndembu of Zambia. This means writing a narrative, a story.

From the first, when contemplating the form of the book, I wanted to reconstruct the anthropological evidence and analysis in my own way, to make it over into the kind of flowing narrative that I saw in it myself. Having been actually there among the Ndembu, I felt that by means of this technique I could give something of the original experience, also allowing it to be colored by carefully developed analysis, which was, after all, our own set of meanings ramifying out of the original material over the years. Thus the story I tell—simplified from the great length of the fieldnotes, changed by years of maturation, different both from an anthropologist's style of reportage and that of his analysis—is aimed to "bring the . . . mutual invention of anthropologist and 'native' alike into awareness," as Roy Wagner puts it in *The Invention of Culture*.

Is the book, then, a novel, a memoir, or an anthropological account? The anthropologists deserve some help to identify the production for their own purposes, and with the help I give below they may be able to decide for themselves. I would like to call it advocacy anthropology in the female style, that is, speaking on behalf of a culture as a lover or a mother. I decided to use all the observations, knowledge, and field material that I and Vic had collected, and form them—these actual facts of fieldwork, not imaginary material—into a coherent story, adding my own blood of motherhood, as it were, to feed the embryo so that it might grow in its own true way.

Now for some general "nuts and bolts" information and some particulars about the use of eyewitness accounts and reported events. As regards the translation of dialogue and Ndembu terms and concepts, the dialogue usually is a rendition into colloquial English of actual conversations. Certain passages, which I list below, are supposed conversations based on knowledge of the circumstances. I have avoided vernacular words as far as possible, using English terms which, it must be stated, can only be approximations of the original. As for chronology, the events refer to our second period of fieldwork, from 1953–54.

The facts about the girl's initiation, Chapter 4, were learned over a period of time and garnered from many repeated experiences of the same type of initiation. This material has been fed into one ritual for the reader's benefit. The initiate's marital night is a reported account; it was carefully researched and is close to the fieldnotes. The story of the boys' circumcision ceremony, Chapter 2, I have reconstructed in the same narrative fashion as the rest of the book, though it refers to events I did not witness. The facts have been checked against Victor Turner's account, and the personal reactions of the characters approximate closely with field reports, which themselves were often on an intimate level. In Chapter 7, the story of Nyamwaha's death, an actual cause célèbre known to all of Kajima, has been fleshed out in keeping with our firsthand experience of similar circumstances.

The description of Nyamuvwila's despair in Chapter 8 is taken from reports of the protagonist's feelings and complaints at the time; likewise, the scenes from the sorcerer's private life and the story of Kavula in Nyamuvwila's hut draw upon the same kind of knowledge. The Thunder Ritual in Chapter 8 is composed mainly of eyewitness material, supplemented for the sake of a flowing story with the information of Ndembu consultants.

Mostly, *The Spirit and the Drum* is an eyewitness account. The characters were all real people; in a few cases where reputations are involved they have been given pseudonyms. The poems on pages 37 and 130–31 are free translations from Ndembu texts. Deviations from texts in Victor Turner's *The Forest of Symbols* and *Revelation and Divination* have been made with an eye to interpretations still in fieldnote form.

If my readers will follow the book as a story they may not only gain anthropological instruction, but also may become involved existentially with the Ndembu, so as to share the impact that the events had on us, along with an understanding of the rich repertoire of meanings that all true religions provide.

My grateful thanks go to the Institute for African Studies, Zambia, (formerly the Rhodes-Livingstone Institute) for providing the original grant that supported us in Africa, and especially for my travel expenses; and to the Wenner-Gren Foundation for Anthropological Research and the Carter Woodson Institute of Afro-American and African Studies at the University of Virginia, which funded my recent return trip to the Ndembu; to Marcia Brubeck, John Casey, and my daughter Rene Wellman, who did considerable editing work on the manuscript; to Beth Goldring, Barbara Babcock, Barbara Myerhoff, Hildred Geertz, and others for their encouragement; to Manyosa, Musona, Samutamba, Muchona, and Windson Kashinakaji, who not only made major contributions to the text but who were very much coauthors of it; and lastly, to Victor Turner, who probed down into the inner workings of Ndembu social and psychological life and into the life of the spirit itself, in hundreds of ways bringing the Ndembu alive—"man and woman alive," as he said, quoting D. H. Lawrence—having first presented the material in a supremely concrete and informed way. Vic was the exemplar of the anthropology of experience, and thus I can say that without him this book would never have been written.

EDITH TURNER
University of Virginia

INTO THE LAND OF THE NDEMBU

THE TRUCK WAS LOADED HIGH. We were traveling three hundred and fifty miles west from the copper towns of Zambia, far from the last blacktop road or department store or telephone wire, almost to the borders of Angola. As we approached the divide, outcrops of rock began to appear. Ahead lay a track that was merely a line through the bush from which the trees and elephant grass had been removed, a road now so unkempt that I asked Vic whether we were going the right way. He nodded. We rose slowly into the upland among bracken and wild apricots and clouds, a landscape that stayed with us for many hours, until the rocks seemed about to end all. Then we emerged on the brow, beyond which sprang up an enormous view, blue as water and wide as the sea. Forest after forest stretched away, and an arm of the Lunga River gleamed in the hollow of the land. The children crowed.

Rene, a gay and confident four-year-old, burst out, "When will we get there, Mommy?"

I gave her a hug. "Not today. We'll have to stay at the rest house in Mwinilunga and arrive at Kajima tomorrow."

The village of Kajima was far on the western border of Zambia, near the sources of the Zambezi and the Congo, the great rivers that flow across Africa in opposite directions. We had come from England for a year's anthropological fieldwork in this little-known village of the Ndembu people. We had already learnt something of the Ndembu, having made a previous trip to the general area, and had picked up hints that there was a deep level of religion and symbolism in their culture. The use of such material might ruin our respectable Marxist stance, but we were going to explore it anyway, believing that nothing human was alien to us.

We were five in the family: Vic and I; Freddy, our freckly son of nine; Bobby, a dark-haired little fellow of six, and Rene.

We drove on, and at last a bridge appeared at the bottom of a steep hill. Vic put the engine into low. Like all the bridges on the route, this one was made entirely of wood: the spanning timbers were floored with a corduroy of smaller logs, which ranged across the bridge from one end to the other. The truck drove up to where the logs started. Two lines of very narrow planks, the only sawed wood in the construction, had been positioned from end to end over the logs to ease the springs of the trucks. Our vehicle mounted the planks, causing the bridge to tremble. I could see out of the side window clear to the bottom of the river. Vic steered the wheels straight, each over its own plank. Judging from the froth on the water below, it was not well-behaved like the rivers at home. Beyond hurtled a waterfall, sweeping into a lower whirlpool in a wide circle of bottle-green controlled water. Over the whirlpool hung sumptuous palms, wild hedges of glittering evergreen leaves, and white trumpets. A wave of delicious scent came up to us. At last we were through to the dirt road, attacking the slope to escape from the dangerous overhang on one side.

Now we could see occasional Africans along the road, young boys, skinny and poorly clad, walking to the town of Mwinilunga. We passed, looking eagerly at them: they looked odd, jiving as they went, resembling inverted question marks. Now the trees that had been a continuous multitude grouped themselves in copses, and the plain of Mwinilunga spread before us, yellow in the great day, peaceful and endlessly wide. The track slithered through it, originally straight but now looped with detours and skidmarks in the sand of the drought. In the distance a herd of duiker antelope bounded away, flickering like birds over the ground. The truck roared on and on through the sand before it finally bounced into the woods, where we immediately found ourselves in inhabited country. Here and there stood groups of villages of a dozen houses or so, two or three to a mile, with banks of cassava hanging over the roadside.

Cassava, the African version of manioc, resembles a field of lupine plants without the flower, bearing hand-like fronds jutting from woody stalks that are ridged around with projections like those of a cheese grater. Set in the countless mounds that fret the underworld of soil, the plants are phenomenal starch-producers; if you dig into the mound after the four years of the plant's life, you find enormous roots cramming the soil. These are the Ndembu's staple food.

As we passed on, a chicken flew across the road in a frenzy. Another village veered by. A neat cottage appeared, all by itself, set back from the road and surrounded by a low hedge of heliotrope. A door stood proudly in the middle of the wall, each panel painted a different color. Someone had daubed the brown plaster on one side with a bold checkering of whitewash. On the other side, one window frame was dramatically outlined in white. The thatch was trimmed with obsessive neatness all around, and the yard was scrupulously swept. A shade tree, the only one among acres of cassava, stood behind the house, near which we glimpsed a pounding mortar and a white drift of cassava flour.

"The house of the agricultural counselor," said Vic, his hand out of the window.

We crossed the wide Lunga bridge and almost at once we were in town, our necks straining this way and that to see if we could recognize the landmarks. There was the store—a mere shack—a whitewashed school, the market, a half-built church, and the mango avenue. An imposing building with a long verandah bore the sign MWINILUNGA DISTRICT OFFICE. We had arrived in Mwinilunga. The District Commissioner was out of town so we returned to the store and piled out of the truck, stiff but triumphant. I stood for a moment pushing back my brown hair, trying to remember my surroundings. The old black storekeeper caught sight of Vic and came waddling out.

"Mr. Turner," he beamed. "It's good to see you again!"

We all shook hands. A few women who were shrinking back observed the warmth of the gesture. They gracefully tucked their babies behind their backs in the carrying cloths, and advanced proudly to greet me, passing the palms of their hands along my palm. "Mwani," they said. "Hi." The backs of the hands, theirs and mine, had the same tendon lines and veins, whether black or white.

We all went into the store. Around three sides ran a counter on which nothing was displayed except a black bicycle inner tube lying crookedly across the side counter, where a long-legged youth in short pants was thrusting out his lips in an ugly fashion, unwilling to agree to the price. He grew open-eyed at the sight of newcomers.

The storekeeper went to his place behind the counter and spread his hands upon it.

"Well, Dona," he said, using the Portuguese courtesy. "What can I do for you?"

I looked up at the sparsely-stocked shelves behind him and chose some provisions: a large can of melon marmalade, unpleasant but better than nothing; a bottle of palm oil, useful in case the order from town arrived late; a can of Cadbury's chocolate, with something we had never seen before, an interior foil seal; Nescafe; a small expensive can of Cowlac dried milk (if only I could be sure of the other order, with large cans of Cowlac in it); matches, which came in a packet of a dozen boxes, still astonishing to our frugal souls; and a carton of cigarettes. The carton, containing five hundred OK's was very cheap. We didn't

buy the *Penny Line* at a penny for eight, because we knew they
destroyed your throat.

We grabbed our bundled purchases before the courteous onlookers could do the carrying for us, which would make us feel
like bwanas. Vic wrenched open the OK carton and plucked out
a bright red packet. He handed the cigarettes around and took
one himself, dropping the empty packet. A small boy saw his
opportunity, and reached out with a respectful arm to salvage
it. The box would be a useful container for his treasures.

We spent the night at the rest house. While waiting for Vic, who
was fixing the truck, I sat on my bed, my feet cold on the polished European floor. Here we were in Mwinilunga again. Last
time I had developed a thirst for fieldwork and was beginning
to realize there was more to life than cooking and baby-minding.
This time I had the chance to explore the depths of a culture. It
could be real work, not the everlasting trick of finding useful
things to do so as to avoid work.

My toes were rebelling against the floor, so I tucked them up
in bed; soon Vic came in and we were able to get cozy together.

The next day we climbed into the truck and took the road for
Kajima, an even bumpier ride than before. At the top of the final
rise we began to see brown thatches hidden among trees. Vic
looked for the right turning, and my heart gave a great squeeze
within me. We drove around the corner, found the next gap
where the village entrance ought to be, and turned into it. The
track was completely overgrown, save for a narrow footpath. Vic
stopped the vehicle and we precipitated out. A young lad stood
looking with a puzzled expression down the path toward us,
then shouted to the rear. We followed him toward the village,
which opened out in a circle of fifteen shabby mud houses. Now
I could see it really was Kajima, the village we knew.

Three children reached us first. "Sakeru!" said Freddy.

"My friend," answered Sakeru, bright and solemn. Sakeru wore an ancient pair of bermudas and a ragged shirt with the buttons missing. He held his head back, with lips protruding and serene. He was obviously trying to control his thin legs and feet, which were starting to dance. The boys walked side by side, the one excited and freckled, the other solemn and black. Women in long waistcloths gathered and came toward us— good old faces now—and they swept their hands up and together and burst out singing. We all went forward in a mass, a song wreathing us about—"Ey-yey-yey! Mama wa lembi, yey-yey!"—in an immediate rich harmonized chorus.

Overcome, I grasped my children's hands and beamed around. We were approaching a rough circular shelter in the middle of the village, beside which stood old Master Kajima in his long waistcloth and jacket, shabby but fine. With him was his second headman, Sakazao. Kajima's face was solemn, but his brown eyes glowed as he welcomed us to the village. "You have reached home! You have reached home!" he pronounced in the traditional words. How could I keep from smiling? I couldn't be solemn like him, I was not an elder and did not have the restraint that comes through certainty of self-expression.

We were led to stools beside the shelter. I looked up and saw our old friend Musona, beaming and excited. He was a younger elder with a long face, twisted now into a boyish grin. Musona was a good translator; he could expatiate on various Ndembu customs and, like all his family, he was a great gossip. He hired himself out to Vic without more ado and became his passionate and jealous follower, as if he owned this unusually intimate white man. Now, greeting us, his eyes danced with hope. We beamed back at him, and he wrung our hands English-fashion, showing us his emotions because he understood our Western ways.

The singing crowd grouped around us, while scores of clapping hands punctuated the rhythm. My hands also moved to clap to that riotous rhythm, and then I remembered that I must keep still: they were singing to us, not we to them. We grew quite tired of sitting, but at last it came time to speak.

"You have surprised us, Mister Vic," said Musona. "Your car has metamorphosed, like a chameleon."

"It's been painted. I just changed the color, see?" Vic took them to the truck and scratched a little of the light brown to show them the blue underneath. "It really is the same car."

At that moment there was a scuffle through the village as one of Kajima's sons chased a chicken. His little legs twinkled and his girl cousin joined in to round up the frantic bird as it circled and circled. The children grabbed it and presented it to Kajima. Kajima bound its legs and took it by the head and feet.

"Greetings, greetings, a chicken," he said, laying it on Vic's knees. Vic looked affectionately into the brown eyes. He held the lively bird down with one elbow and clapped twice. He and Kajima shook hands, and then each clasped his hand around the other's thumb, then a handshake, then two claps. It was the original unabbreviated black soul shake in its home territory. As for the bird, Musona freed it to lay eggs for us.

I was suddenly conscious of my fatigue. Heaps of baggage lay on the ground beside the truck and all of them would have to be brought into the village somehow, so I picked up the blankets and staggered along. Musona approached and asked, "What about flour? No flour?"

"Oh, whatever—we'll eat the bread and margarine we brought with us," I answered impatiently. I leaned over the bedding, trying to untie the camp cots and thinking, "What a shabby village—it's just a dump. Look at that old animal skull left by a tree." Vic came by and put another box down. In a low voice I said to him, "I'm not sure about this village. Couldn't we go and live in Chibwika? Didn't you say there might be more interesting rituals there? There'd be a lot of wild game."

"I've got a hunch about Kajima. We already know the people

here, so we won't have much difficulty about sitting in on their doings. Trust me." He headed back to the truck for a fresh load of bags.

I sighed, aware of both my misgivings and my exhaustion. He was right, of course.

When the boxes were shifted I called the children together and looked for a way out of the village. Perhaps we could explore the overgrown trails around Kajima.

For a long time we wandered, picking our way through frowsty yellow grass matted into paths. Suddenly I hesitated and drew the children back. Turds lay here and there before me, and I saw the reason for these paths that led nowhere. They had been created so that the villagers could take a comfortable crap without grass tickling their buttocks. Hearing a buzz, I looked down. I had stopped none too soon, for a large winged beetle was folding her wings beside a fresh turd in the middle of the path. The children crowded around as the beetle set to work, scrabbling about on her prize with powerful legs. Soon she had detached a manageable portion. Forgetting my distaste in my fascination, I too crouched down to watch.

The beetle poised on her portion of dung and shaped it into a perfect globe. Then, descending, she pushed on it backwards to roll it off the path to a patch of softer soil. There she dug a hole into which she lowered the dung. After a moment's pause, she laid an egg beside her globe of nourishment.

I pointed at the beetle's head. "See those projections, like the rays of the sun? She's the sacred Egyptian scarab. They used to carve scarabs as a symbol of resurrection and immortality. She buries the whole world and a new beetle is resurrected from the grave." I pondered this connection. Our intelligence, if as good as this remarkable beetle's, could bring about resurrection from dung again and again—it was a matter of using the earth's resources rightly.

The beetle, having done her work, flew away, and we returned to Kajima. There in the middle stood the umbrella tent, erected by Musona and his men in our absence. It was late afternoon and a slight breeze blew into the flaps. In the coolness inside stood a table—not ours. It was spread with a clean towel, on which was set a golden brown chicken surrounded by roast potatoes and gravy.

"Wow!" exclaimed the boys. "This is fine." Freddy put his hands at each end of the table and admired it.

"Musona lent us that table," said Vic, entering.

"That's very decent of him," I said. "Another chicken. Where did this one come from?"

"Itota, the old hunter from up the road. He gave it to me while I was unloading. He came through and left at once; he's not used to society. Musona cooked the chicken while you were out."

Vic had already renewed his friendships, then; it was surely that gift for rapport he had developed in the army. I now felt an affection for this village with its good manners and generous neighbors. We pulled boxes and footlockers up to the table and sat down. Surely no one could roast potatoes quite like Musona; the gravy was almost painfully tasty.

It was still our first evening in Kajima, and now it was about time the children were in bed. I settled them down in the umbrella tent, which I now saw had a six-inch tear in the side. Rene, Freddy, and Bobby soon discovered the hole and sprang up continually to peep through the dewy canvas at the comings and goings outside. In the east the moon was rising beyond the twelve-foot anthill that dominated the houses—beyond the night soil path, beyond the trees, actually far away over the plain.

By the time our children had grown quiet, the scene at Kajima had changed. Bright gray light poured into the village as if from distant floodlighting. Children from every house ran about under the brilliant medallion, their black heads bobbing, figures leaping, with much giggling and laughter. While I watched, a few started to circle around an object—a shrine or a pineapple cactus—twisting and jiving as they circled. Their harsh voices sang a popular tune, skillfully harmonized. Spellbound, I listened to the art of the impromptu blending of parts—a lost art in the West, except among blacks and specially trained groups. Around and around they danced. Then they broke up and formed another circle for a game with the older girls and women. A senior woman entered the group and began to teach them, while they listened respectfully. She set them going with the right tune and then stood outside the circle, while they put the headman's teenage daughter, Mwenda, into the center. Now they crouched close around Mwenda, all holding hands. Louder and louder grew the song, while gradually the whole circle rose up on its feet, gathering in closer still upon Mwenda. The song reached a climax, and Mwenda in the middle rose to a dizzying height above them all—how, I couldn't make out—and then fell. Fascinated, they played this game again and again. And fascinated, I watched.

In a flash they started another game. For this one, they sat on their heels in a circle. Someone sang a gentle trilling solo that was answered in a rollicking chorus. Next, two children in alternate positions swiftly knelt upright and nodded to each other over the child in between, afterwards subsiding while the child in between nodded to the next alternate child, and so on around the circle until each child had nodded to a partner. The game was rhythmically and surely played, except for two boys who weren't watching out and who muffed their turns. They were pushed out of the circle and jeered at by the quicker-witted girls, but they crept back in as soon as they could.

Again they stood in a circle holding hands. One of the children lowered her hand, still holding her neighbor's, and stepped over the hands, one foot at a time. She kept firm hold of her neighbors' hands on both sides, and when she stood with her two feet outside the ring she ducked her head under one of her neighbor's hands to untwist herself. Each child took a turn at this, right around the circle.

Next a buxom young wife called Kandaleya took command. She sent a couple of boys off, and they returned with three smooth pounding poles about seven feet long and four inches thick. She placed these on the ground to form the letter H, with the transverse pole rolling unsteadily on top of the other two. Kandaleya stood on this and they all sang. She wobbled and twisted, while they alternately jeered and trilled their tongues in praise; then she danced some steps. Soon she was doing a complicated dance routine, crossing her feet on either side of the pole and back again on top of it. The boys started to jog the end poles. Kandaleya shrieked out but stayed on. They all trilled and shouted, "Nkinga! Bicycle, bicycle, bicycle!" This game is also played in Hawaii, but why it occurs in such widely separated regions is one of anthropology's conundrums.

A game of propellor whirl followed. Three children sat on the ground in a circle facing inwards, their legs spread out in front of them with all the heels touching in the center. Three other children stood between them and gripped their hands. The whole circle began to whirl around as the vertical children spun, lifting the others slightly off the ground. The song went, "Flying, can't you see me flying!"

Another game resembled "Oranges and Lemons." A long line formed, and all went under an arch made by the arms of two big boys in front. The big boys trapped each child in turn as he passed under the arch. As each one was caught the whole group sang: "Who's the witch? Smell him out!" The child was set on the joined arms of the boys and they asked him: "Who's your sweetheart?" When he answered, the boys thumped him down, shouting in half-broken voices, "Let's break open this old calabash," and everyone shrieked with laughter.

Not long before the end came a curious game without a winner. Like all the games it was a kind of kinesthetic exercise and drama. The children formed a long string, holding hands. The leader drew the string after him and ducked under the arms of the last two in the line, and the rest followed until the line had turned inside out. Then all went under the arms of the next to the last pair, then under the arms of the children next to them, and so on, singing,

> When I die
> they'll bury me
> all alone
> in a woodland grave,
> I'll leave my brother
> far away,
> oh, how lonesome
> I will be.

All followed the leader "into the grave," joining with the mourners to become mourners themselves, just as neighbors do at an Ndembu funeral. In the next verse the words changed: they sang, "We follow like a flock of chicks." The leader shouted, "To Mother Hen!" I looked on broodingly, conscious of the sadness and affection of this game, thinking how much they enjoyed being together, here in the forest where lives were so short.

The last game I can hear even now. The tune is African, but some of the words appear to be Portuguese in origin:

> Ve-ve-ve-ve, Marīng-ina,
> Ve-ve-ve-ve, Marīng-ina,
> Ey, Maringina, ey Maringina
> Ey, Maringina, ey Maringina.
> Mwana story, mwana story, fida pe.

Mwana means "child." They all sat around, leaning forward and placing their hands palms down on the ground in a neat circle. The song ended with the refrain: "Count, count, count, count!" while the leader tapped each brown hand in turn. The last one tapped had to be turned upward, so that one hand in the circle looked white (southern Africans have white palms). This was repeated until some child had both palms turned upward and was put out of the game. Eventually all were eliminated in this way. The last one jumped up in a rush and chased all the rest, for he was now the "hyena." The others scattered in a panic, each one sitting down to draw a circle in the sand around him representing his hut. Those who didn't draw a circle in time were "eaten up." After this game the whole junior membership of the village gathered for a terrific romp, and the evening was over.

I sighed and looked for Vic. In the men's shelter I saw Vic get off his stool; in the glowing radiance from the fire his hand appeared in silhouette, passing round a last share of cigarettes. There was a growl of farewell. He ducked and emerged from under the low roof, then stumbled over in the darkness to our tent. We found a candle and closed the flap. Here we were in our new home, glad to sink down on our camp cots.

"Didn't I tell you?" said Vic, his hands behind his head. "My hunch is going to work out. What a welcome, eh?"

"I know." I was thinking about the whole day's events, my ups and downs of feeling. "We've been shown some real courtesy. Do you think we'll be able to teach our own kids such courtesy?"

Vic laughed. "Let's try; we European savages have a lot to learn."

As I fell asleep I was thinking what fun Western children could have if they played those games.

In the next few days I met Musona's queenly wife Mangaleshi and his five children. There were twelve–year–old Sani and her beautiful sister Diana. These girls wore simple shifts. There were Jerry "Who-Resembled-His-Dad," Monica the toddler, who wore nothing but a short grayish dress, and the newborn baby, Betty. Monica screamed naughtily when Betty lay on her mother's lap. With a mean expression on her face she would edge herself on to the lap along with Betty, and then try to push Betty off. Mangaleshi looked at Monica with a tired experienced smile.

Sakazao the second headman, broad in every way, used to amble around in a long white waistcloth, with a sly comfortable look on his face. He was one of the few non-sorcerers in the village. Then, too, I became reacquainted with Samutamba, who was a sorcerer. I remembered how we used to stop on the road by his large house on the previous trip. Samutamba would be there with a cabbage, or a chicken, or some corn on the cob. He was the Humphrey Bogart type, ugly to look at, but with a heart-catching charm when a smile broke on his face.

This is the scene by the road: Samutamba has heard the truck from afar while at his farm, and he hurries to the road. There he stands, thinking, "Is that Mr. Vic?" His heart melts. He thinks of that hateful village, Kajima; will Mr. Vic help him to become headman? His brow lowers and his jaw widens into a dangerous scowl; his willful shoulders, bow legs, and long upper head all look hideous. Here he is at his own fine farm, and that's where the center of the village ought to be. Never mind the Kajima people, he would force his wives to help him with his gardens, to earn cash. And again and again he would couple with them to beget children. But he curses—there is always this vile disease (it was gonorrhea). Ah, but here comes the truck, bearing his old cobber from the other end of the world. (Nothing can beat these cross-color friendships.) His eyes light up like tots of rum, he is gay, broad, and delighted. His whole face turns about like a ship approaching the harbor. Then the smile appears, like the Union Jack breaking from the masthead, and we bounce up in the car and cheer. Samutamba's eyes glitter. His grin is almost terrifying; in fact, he looks around as if he might be arrested for so much fun. But his head goes back in pride as he presents the corn cobs, pushing them unceremoniously into the car, allowing no thanks, and stands back waving and straddling about until the car disappears. And this man is a sorcerer.

We lived in the center of Kajima Village along with nine related families, who entered our lives more and more. At night we heard Musona shouting from within his house to his older sister Manyosa within her hut two doors away, and we could hear Manyosa's indignant counter-remarks. This village was like one great house owned by one extended family, with the sky roofing its minor units.

The rectangular thatch on the larger type of hut was curved like the tilt in a farm boy's straw hat. The peak of the roof crested like a cock's comb, high and gallant; then the roof swept down and rested, poised wide, on verandah struts. It sheltered a simple box with red clay walls. In the heart of the walls was a skeleton of wattle that showed through here and there, a thin web of sticks cut long ago from the bush and now smelling of old dry mud.

The odd circle of huts seemed to parade around the shelter in the center of the plaza. The shelter was the men's meeting place, in a sense, their pub; it was called the chota, a much-used word. It was merely a wide cone of thatch, a round straw hat set on posts with a log fire inside and, to sit on, a log or two, an ancient deck chair, and an African stool for the headman. You could smell the soot in the old thatch; the posts were dark and rubbed shiny. Inside, the buzz of conversation never ceased; there were always two or three men settled comfortably, talking in shifting sporadic voices about taxes, prices, land, children, sickness— barefoot men, their lean bodies clad in old shirts and bermudas, some sitting on the ground, their knees stuck up by their ears as they listened. If a lawcase were in progress, everyone would attend, both to judge the case and to savor the skillful rhetoric.

Headman Kajima was on his stool. His face rested in its habitual expression of reticent kindliness. Kajima knew he was the embodiment of the village and he refused to exert a strong personality to blur that fact. He sat paring a mango, handing the slivers of fruit to his grandsons. They liked it and kept putting out their hands for more.

By now I had learned the story of the old animal skull by the tree. It was the skull of a water buffalo, the most dangerous animal in Africa, and on second examination I saw that it was placed by a shrine in the vicinity of an ancestor tree, one whose sap ran like tears. The shrine itself was a tiny straw shelter set up on long poles, in which hung a bag containing the tooth of the hunter Lupinda, Kajima's ancestor.

In the men's hut it was told how Master Kajima killed the buffalo ten years ago, having come across his trail leading into the mud of the Kakula River valley; how Kajima had lined up his sights seconds before the buffalo turned to look at him; how he had to aim for the artery on the side of the neck—the front of the head was invulnerable, protected by one solid mass of horn and bone, which was easy to see when you tilted up the skull and felt the thickness across the brow. The buffalo had only to face Kajima for the hunter's chances to be nil. He fired, and the bullet tore a hole in the jugular. A dead shot, Kajima; and now in the chota he was honored as the holder of the highest rank in the hunters' guild.

Far off, the women laughed in a sudden clatter of voices. They were aware of what went on in the chota as they worked in their open kitchens, sitting cross-legged with their waistcloths drawn up discreetly between their legs. In their mission garb the sexy girls still looked sexy and the laughing ones were still able to beckon a shoulder suggestively. Mwenda and Sani, who were friends, rushed about, occasionally striking elegant poses to express anger at each other. Cries and calls floated across the village: Sano! Mwendo! Musono! Singing constantly burst forth in an infectious rhythm as someone pounded cassava, the children took to dancing around a pineapple plant, or as they imitated my call to Freddy—"Lach*tayim* Fe*di*" (Lunchtime, Freddy), "Ka-*mon* Fe*di*" (Come on, Freddy)—in a syncopated tune from the top of an anthill.

One night while Vic was in the chota with the men, I heard a cheerful company of women approach my tent. A black hand grasped the flap; it was Manyosa.

"We've come for a chat as you're all by yourself, Mishy," she explained.

"Come in, great to see you. Ingila mwani," I said, no longer bored, and I moved up along the camp cot to leave space. In came Manyosa around the flap, her long face alight with curiosity. We greeted, both goggling a little with pleasure. After her came Mangaleshi, benevolent and gracious, then Mesala wearing a delighted grin. She was the clown of the village. A white Mishy's tent was likely to be a real joke. She entered, stumbling about—"Eh! Eh!" in a gritty wide voice, "and where do I sit?" She collapsed on my camp cot, which rocked alarmingly. That was enough. We were all roaring with laughter, Manyosa and Mangaleshi with pitying expressions, Mesala one hundred percent. She was broad of face and bonny, a face impossible to focus because her mouth, eyes, and cheeks were always moving. (A little boy looking with wonder at his unsheathed penis was enough to send Mesala off into peals. The others would look away but smile behind their hands.)

At this point I found myself speaking Ndembu in a kind of wild way and having a good time. The women told me they would like me to come to the kitchens every evening, "for the chatting." I did so and learnt to relish the relaxed atmosphere in the darkness, the voices over the little bit of fire, and the final yawns as we tottered off to bed.

Manyosa's kitchen was a square shelter with a few side posts and a thatch, a place where you could spread a mat on the dirt floor and lean against a post. One day I ducked under the roof while she was cooking to greet her with the caressing of palms.

"Greetings, mwani." She resumed her stirring. "Glad you've come, Mishy, because my grandchild is visiting today. Mpeza, that's her name; she's the finest baby in the world, and she's going to grow up just like her grandmother."

Her long ancient wraparound skirt caught my eye as it stretched over her buttocks by the fire, or wrinkled when she rapidly turned around with her brows raised, looking for a plate and continuing her conversation with me. She spoke Ndembu crisply like an orator, the speech of a peasant. She was describing Mpeza's birth.

Now Rosina, Manyosa's daughter, came up at her mother's imperious call, walking quietly so as not to disturb the sagging bundle on her back. Rosina sat down with exquisite grace and loosened her carrying cloth to bring the baby around to the front. I sat looking at Rosina. A rose she was, the dark red kind, with that gentle fold in the cheek line, and lips everted like the petals of certain flowers that strain backwards. Her small cousins crowded around. Mwenda the teenager took the baby carefully from Rosina on to her own lap and played with her, clapping her fat hands, curling her silky black hair, pushing her lips into a pout. How they love that baby, I thought; they spoil her.

"Mishy, come here," whispered Manyosa. She took out from under the thatch a goat's horn stuffed with a black substance. "Rosina's medicine horn. Just after the baby was born Rosina bled badly." Manyosa's hand clutched me. "We had to perform an exorcism."

Gradually she managed to tell the story. I myself pass it on recreated in my own way and filled out with details learned from Vic. The exorcism was directed against a certain snake familiar bred by a certain sorcerer; it was a long occult rite, frightening to everybody. Darkness was falling in Kajima when Rosina lay in a flooding hemorrhage. The whole village rose in terror.

Manyosa dashed past the chota shouting, "Neglect! Neglect!" Her arm swung straight toward Samutamba Farm. "You know whom I mean, and none of you men will raise a finger!"

There was a bitter silence.

"My child!" she cried. Her voice rose. "My child is going!"

A neighbor, Sakawumba, said quietly, "Wait, Manyosa. I am a doctor against sorcerers. Show me the girl."

They took him to Rosina's house and pulled back the blanket. Many cloths were bunched between the new mother's legs, soaked with blood. Rosina's face was withered. They saw her fingers move toward the baby, who was squalling angrily.

"The baby! Warm the baby, Manyosa," advised Sakawumba. Manyosa gathered the little creature in her arms.

Sakawumba gazed at the work of sorcery that he discerned in Rosina's fading eyes. He tried hard to recall the proper procedures. He had been in contact with a variety of foul spirits and it had marked his face with the same fear and concern that a psychiatrist feels before severe psychosis. He would have to go to the extreme; it would have to be at once, that night.

Controlling his dread he took his men down to the graveyard. In the pitch darkness they located a grave by the feel of the bare soil. They dug, aiming to find a leg bone in the wormy mess. When the stink made it impossible to go on they forced themselves to picture Rosina as they had just seen her. At last Sakawumba's hand contacted the right bone, a tibia; he drew it out, treating it carefully: it was going to be a gun. Taking it to one side, he stuffed into it slivers of bone and powerful medicines from his wallet, packing them down with scraps of testicle and liver, the organs of strength. The men gathered around in the darkness, and Sakawumba sang his occult verses while they chanted the reply. Squatting, he rotated on his heels and aimed the bone until it pointed in the direction of the brick farm by the road. "Pa-a!" Could he hear a report? Far away an explosion occurred in an invisible python that was crushing Rosina's life.

They returned to Kajima and bore Rosina on a litter down to the Kakula River, all the while playing on sacred rattles. A black goat was the next requirement, evil-eyed and strong-smelling. They held it down to the ground beside the flowing water while they sliced with a knife into the arteries under the neck. When the blood came pumping out Sakawumba held a pot to the artery and filled it. This was strength, ngovu. The drums burst forth, and hoarse singing began, while they sprinkled into the pot particles of the ironwood tree, then gave the potion to Rosina as she lay in collapse. All night long they played the drums, their voices calling the good spirits.

In the morning Rosina began to gain ground. When they carried her back home they took a different route through the bush, avoiding the large house; and when they arrived they found she was peacefully asleep on the litter. The hemorrhage had stopped.

Another day in my explorations I crept around behind Manyosa's house, avoiding the overhanging thatch, and came upon three dirty wrecks of houses, one of which was the hovel once occupied by Nyachitela, "Mother of a Grudge," known as the witch of Kajima. In the space between the huts stood a dead hunter's shrine, a peeled forked stick set in the ground and hung with animal skulls. It belonged to Chikasa, Manyosa's husband, a squeaky-voiced little man who was himself a hunter. Nearby was an ancestor stump that had failed to leaf as it should. Another of the shacks was Manyosa's previous kitchen, stricken by white ants and now sagging; the third was Chikasa's forge, a mere shelter over an ash heap, with leather bellows, hammer, tongs, and a flat granite rock, black and greasy, that served as an anvil. Chikasa had several skills.

As I wandered on, my foot connected with a fragment of litter. It was one–half of a dirty celluloid baby doll, pinkish, long since split down the middle. Just as I bent over it, a figure appeared behind me. It was Nyachitela herself, who from some vantage point in Samutamba Farm where she now lived must have caught sight of me nosing around. She reached past me and picked up the half–doll.

"Heh! A witch-object!" She giggled at its pink half-smile and cackled incontinently. One of her familiars was a living half-hare. This half–doll could become another. "Half-Hare, Half-Hare, Walking Half-Hare! Enter their house, eat their souls, kill!" she sang to herself, turning the half–doll over and over in her bony hands.

She tapped me conspiratorially on the shoulder, chattered like a monkey, and made off. I looked after her, remembering the lurid tales told about her witchcraft. She was a widow and a typical member of the Malabu lineage of Kajima, who were round-faced people with rabbity teeth and sly characters. The headman's lineage, the Nyachintangas, were by contrast long-faced and ambitious.

The gossips told how Nyachitela had eaten the soul of her husband twenty years before, and was now haunted by his ghost, another mode of the spirit. So many deaths had been attributed to her and to the beings clustered around her—indeed, they provoked the very village dogs to bark whenever she passed—that she had been forced to flee to Samutamba Farm. Nevertheless I rather liked Nyachitela. I liked the sizzling canards that she loosed upon some weaker sister, I liked the upward angle of her chin. She didn't exist just as a scapegoat for society's bad feelings, induced by some inconsistency of the social structure. Nyachitela was an actual person. Nor did she represent an object you ought to get rid of, but she was a living being, herself, there.

The witch had gone home. Here behind Manyosa's house was an immense anthill, the home of a fiendish hunter spirit called Mukaala. The hill had grown gloomy pinnacles of clay, among which a misshapen thorn tree straggled upward. From the branches of the tree the fiend was said to peer and whistle and drive away the game. These anthills, often used by hunters to spot game, were the result of the labors of millions of termites. Vic occasionally broke off one of the projecting towers to look inside. There would be a frenzy of movement, the withdrawal of myriads of little heads, revealing the complex honeycombing with its chambers full of eggs, and many intricate passages. Even as he watched the wrecked city, the broken defenses were reinforced by female warriors, creatures bearing huge nipping claws on their heads, which they turned toward the foe like guns in gun turrets. Vic withdrew his hand. As if at a signal, another breed appeared, sturdy workers, each bearing in her mouth a glistening load of wet clay which, after a little investigation, she placed where the break in the wall was lowest. When Vic went to look at the break the next day, the damage was completely repaired.

A trail led out from Manyosa's corner, threading far away through trees into vast plots of cassava that formed a garden one mile long. Beside it ran the main road, merely a dirt road, but something great in these parts. Samutamba was the captain of the road gang for this stretch, and his wives had planted the gardens to feed the roadmen.

The sight of the path saddened me because Samutamba had trodden it for years, long before he built his brick house; he had labored on his vast garden so that he could be wealthy, to make up for the spirits of Kajima denying him children. The irony was that while he attributed his sterility to these spirits he had caught his clap in town, but had nevertheless allied himself with town ways by becoming a wage earner, a cash crop grower, and the owner of a brick farm. He was busy carrying out his strategies, determined to be headman by the accumulation of power; meanwhile he would rule in hell rather than serve in the heaven of insignificance under old Kajima.

At the forest's edge, huge virgin trees had been bitten through by Samutamba's ax and had hurtled to the ground. Their giant limbs lay across the vision everywhere, not yet burned for ash manure. How could he drag them into heaps with no sons to help him?

I walked on through the cassava, in the shade of the dark jointed stalks and fingery fronds, until I came out onto the sand of the roadside drainage channels. The road lay dead straight for one mile, plotted by the district surveyor, a cruel sight in contrast to the cassava fields.

June brought the bitter season of the year, with its cold dew and hot shaky mornings. Then it was that I caught malaria. The illness, suppressed though it was by quinine, proved to have a disturbing core, for the memory of it still makes me anxious. Malaria can recur even when the victim is away from sources of infection. In my case I suffered from the return of anxiety rather than the return of the parasite in the blood.

Hot though it seemed, it was winter; the days were gusty and bright, with impatient whirlwinds shaking the village every now and then, lifting the door of the umbrella tent where I lay sick, almost turning the tent inside out with a fearful rattle of ropes. The nights were still and cold after an orange sunset, and dew sprang into being on every object under the night sky.

I had been lying in the dark, trying to get warm, with the malaria parasite multiplying in my bloodstream for the third time. I had been too ill to peg down the sides of the tent, so that the canvas flopped on the ground, eroded by termites and reddened with their mud. For a long time I lay listening to the village until the bickering died down in the chota and the crisp irritated voices were gone. Suddenly the fever rose in me.

My head swam and I tried to sleep in a dizzy sweaty state. A wind whirled around the tent with a rattle of all the flaps. My eyes were tightly shut; I even found myself clutching the top of the bedclothes to keep them on. To cap it a quarrel started just outside. What were they doing, those people, shouting and arguing? They were quarreling all around my tent! Some interminable argument seemed to go on all night, around and around. The people were small and ugly, with cynical faces; each one seemed just on the point of turning to accuse me. The veiled charges grew deadlier and deadlier, while all around the tent the flaps rose and clapped down like suction cups. I desperately raised my head and forced my eyes to open.

The candle shone over the peaceful tent. Its flame was steady and quite calm. The flaps were hanging still. I rose shakily and, peeping out of the door slit, saw the long stretches of sand and the huts of the village circle, which appeared as usual, dark, lonely, dew-soaked. There was no one there. I turned back and pulled up the shoulder straps of my nightdress where they had fallen. A deep breath stepped through the levels of my lungs until they were full once more.

"They hadn't been quarreling," I said to myself, still anxious, my hand already on the quinine bottle. I pressed the bitter pill down by the root of my tongue and swallowed, then went back to bed.

The next day a sad little deputation of women poured into my tent.

"Mwani, mwani." Manyosa's face smiled at me, sane and healthy. They were all there. I raised my head feebly from the pillow and they gathered around my bed.

"Mishy!" cried Mesala the clown. "We thought you'd gone underground in your tent. Doing a mole act, eh?"

"There goes Mesala again." And they all laughed.

"We've been pretty dull without you," said Manyosa, pouting.

"Hey, give me a chance, will you?" I raised myself on my elbow. Manyosa put a hand on my arm. "Listen. This sickness means something. Kutachika wakata."

"What's that again?"

"It means, 'You start by being sick.' Everyone knows that when you first arrive in a place, you catch whatever's going about. But the secret meaning is, when a spirit wants to catch you, it'll first make you sick. Then if you take notice of what the spirit wants from you, and let it enter you and change you, it will tell you the right way of doing things, from inside, whether it's gardening or hunting or doctoring."

"Thank you, Manyosa." I couldn't think how her words might be true, but it began to work in me.

As soon as I could after my recovery I spread white insecticide powder around the tent, both for mosquitoes and termites. A headman from Chibwika looked down at me tolerantly. He was just straddling the ropes, approaching the entrance of the tent to greet Vic, who was working inside.

"Mpemba, eh?" he asked. Mpemba was the sacred blessing-powder made of white clay, which was used to keep out witches' familiars.

"Yes, sort of," I nodded, a little confused. He seemed pleased with my zeal.

"Have you had trouble with witchcraft familiars?" he asked. I thought he was rather nosey, but replied, "You mean little men who go around and around, accusing you?"

"Why, Mishy, those are the ones. Tuyebela. Did you see them?" He looked back nervously toward Nyachitela's house in Samutamba Farm.

"Oh, no," I lied, persuading myself that it was only the loss of blood cells and the effect of fever on the brain that had caused my nightmare, and not the wrangling bitter tongues, the evil in human beings.

"Come," he said, taking my arm. "I can see what's the matter. If you find you can't stand it here, take up your tent and come to Chibwika. That is a good area with plenty of bush meat. No one there wants to kill people for food."

I shuddered, now half believing that what I had experienced was in fact a brush with the occult, that the little men were sent by Nyachitela to feed on my blood cells in some work of mo-tiveless malignancy. I gratefully shook the hand of my visitor, accepting the offer for some indefinite future time, and returned to my job of completing the magic powder line.

Not long afterwards, Yana's baby Phoebe fell ill. Yana belonged to the Malabu lineage and was here on a protracted visit. We heard her soothing the child at night in a crowded little hut just behind our tent. The Ndembu word for soothing has something of the idea of deception involved in it; kudimbeka meant humoring or cossetting the baby, or diverting its attention to something else. Yana seemed to mock her child: when Phoebe let out a painful pulsating yell, Yana answered with a rhythmic descending "ah-ah-ah-ah," as if she were shaking the breath out of Phoebe. Phoebe kept crying, regardless, with the mother responding, all through the small hours of the night. We discovered that the tiniest babies, just three weeks old, learned to cry rhythmically with such training.

I was summoned to see what the trouble was. I held a thermometer under the delicate brown tortoise-wrinkled armpit, but even before I read the figure, 104°, I could feel the weary heat of the fever. A wee broad-faced child of the Malabus, Phoebe coughed and struggled to breathe; it was bronchitis. I still had a few antibiotics with me, so I broke a pill and mixed half the bitter powder with a spoonful of melon marmalade. Phoebe soon swallowed the marmalade, and I stood by as her doctor, administering half a pill every four hours. Gradually the fever disappeared and the nightly mocking noise ceased.

After that, Yana's hut didn't seem to infringe on our privacy as it had before. The shy husband, also visiting his wife's people, would look out and greet us. Samawika, their son, went out hunting with Bobby. Their smaller daughter, highly intelligent like that branch of the Malabus and now a friend of Rene's, happened to be stone deaf. Dora spoke in gestures, for they were teaching her sign language; she looked out from two enormous eyes with a dazzling hunger for information. Her head was unusually large and her hair was reddish and sparse like the peppercorn hair of a bushman; she was smaller than Rene and was able to wear Rene's outgrown clothing.

Eventually we understood the reason for the condition of her hair and the strange size of her head. She suffered from kwashiorkor, malignant malnutrition. She had been starved of protein titbits at mealtimes because she was deaf and therefore useless. Now she hungrily drank the dried milk we made up for her whenever our children had theirs; and as she and Rene were both learning languages and were both a little cut off, they became great friends. It was hard to believe that Dora was twelve, while Rene was only five.

One day Rene came into Kajima with a bowl in her hand. It was full of caterpillars, which she and Diana had been collecting for relish. They were green caterpillars with black stripes. The children proceeded to stew them until they had produced a noisome black concoction. Dora approached them questioningly.

"Go away, Dora," said Diana, pushing her off. Rene went after Dora and fed her caterpillars like a bird. Dora's face was one big smile.

Several weeks after Phoebe's illness, Yana came to see me with another tiny child holding onto her hand, a child we hadn't seen much of. She leaned toward him as she walked, companioning him, and set him down close beside her under a tree whose roots made clean places to sit.

"This is Sme," said Yana, her face alight with frankness.

Sme? It seemed a strange name. Sme almost disappeared into his mother's clothes, from which two large dirty feet thrust forth. On one ankle was a huge granulated ulcer.

I looked at Yana. "You have come for medicine, then?" I lifted Sme's foot. I was uneasy. Wasn't this the sort of ulcer that turned cancerous? Peering at the seeping mess, I saw that at least it could be cleansed and protected from the dust, and I went to fetch bandages. Yana was pulling at Sme's hand, commanding him to be quiet. I dressed the sore and gave Sme an enormous bandaging with strips torn from old sheets, wrapping a thick wad all over his foot to keep out the dust. Sme was quite miserable.

As I put the materials away I thought, "His legs are very thin."

I took another look out of the tent. They were just getting to their feet. I observed that Sme's brow was high and narrow and his face was gnome-like from starvation. I had an evanescent vision of the hyena-ridden rocks on the way to Sme's home in the north. It was a lonely village, far from any source of wages, by a sandy plain where blacksmiths used to feed a sacred smelting furnace. Knowing that the ulcer would heal better if Sme had extra protein, I went to the kitchen shelter, where biltong was strung across the roof, and unwrapped some of the dark red leathery pieces of antelope meat from the string. Then I ran after Sme and gave him the scraps.

"Come again tomorrow," I told him. He tumbled away on his club of bandages, desperate to escape me.

Yana brought him constantly. Very gradually he took to smiling slightly when I plumped the meat into his lap. Very slowly the sore dried at the edges and ebbed into a smaller and smaller area. At last I learned his real name, Siměo Nyakumesa, or, as he was called affectionately by the village, Nyak'maisa. Yana had given us his Portuguese name out of politeness.

Chautongi's toddler Kandemba, slightly younger than Nyakumesa, became his friend and accompanied him for quinine when Nyakumesa came for dressings. Later on, both received dried milk instead of meat. In the darkness at suppertime, when the pressure lamp roared defiantly at the flies and moths, there would be a small sound outside, and we would stop talking.

"There they are," Vic said, and our children grinned knowingly.

"Yitumbu," came the clear little voice. Medicine.

Outside the door stood two small upright figures, Nyakumesa and Kandemba, looking way up at me with the fondest expressions. They put out their hands, and I touched them with the greeting of passing friends. Then I gave them their foaming cups of milk. They drank them down like soldiers, presented me with the cups as if they were chalices, and ran off chattering distinctly all the way to their mommies' houses.

Then, too, the son of Mbimbi, an old man who lived between us and the road, fell seriously ill. We heard the distant thud of drums beyond the trees, and not long afterward Manyosa called us from our tent. She led us to Mbimbi's village, lit that night by an enormous fire fully forty feet across and criss-crossed by white-hot tree trunks. We approached the fire and retreated: it was like a sun of raging hydrogen, hollow in its airy heat.

Mbimbi's name meant "funeral master." Despite his age—and he looked as if he had existed since the earliest days of humanity—he was huge and strong. Now, in the heavy folds of his face dwelt a passion which nobody could approach. On cracked bare feet Mbimbi had dragged the logs out of the forest and filled the center of the village with them; Mbimbi was afraid, with the energy of panic.

The villagers sat on logs in a wide ring around the fire, singing hoarsely. Desperation was in the air. From time to time heads turned anxiously to watch something outside the circle. I looked, but saw nothing, then noticed a peculiar shape fluttering in the shadows. It was an owl. The bird ran just beyond the circle, sometimes on the ground, sometimes flying up to perch on the houses, hooting all the time.

Manyosa and I shuddered together. "That is the witchcraft familiar," she said. "See how close it comes. It's Nyachitela's, for sure, and she's sent it to kill Mbimbi's son." Her lip curled. "She'll eat him, Mishy." I stared at the creature, wondering why it dared to come so close to people.

At that moment Musona tapped me on the shoulder and beckoned me to come and look at the boy where he lay in his special enclosure.

"He's not breathing right," Musona explained as we walked along.

"Perhaps it's pneumonia," I thought to myself.

The clearing was as bright as day, lit by the towering fire. Mbimbi came over, his jaw set, and joined us. We peered into the enclosure. The child lay curled up on a litter, sheltered by the matting walls. Nervously reaching into my bag, I found some medicine and poured it into a spoon. Then I stepped through the entrance. A second too late I saw an object on the ground at my feet, an African medicine pot balanced atop a tiny squared-off stake driven into the ground. Even as I realized what it was, my foot collided with it, upsetting the pot and its precious liquid. At the same moment my spoon tilted and the European medicine flowed down my skirt. A cold fear entered the enclosure with me; that's that, it seemed to say.

Bending down, I felt the child's brow and saw that his teeth were set tight.

"It's the rock-hyrax disease," Musona said in a low voice. "From the coney, the chibatata. The coney clenches its teeth and chatters—batatatata—that noise. The disease is very dangerous: the boy will not open his teeth now."

I leaned the rigid boy up on my arm and turned him this way and that, trying to prise open his teeth so that he could take medicine. The child lay chained by his own muscles, slowly being throttled. Suddenly I recognized the symptoms.

"Lockjaw! Tetanus. Did he have a wound infected with dirt?"

No one knew. I was facing real trouble. I put the boy's head down gently and turned. "Can't we get him to the hospital? We should try."

Headman Mbimbi looked at his own pillar-like legs, skin-ridged like the hide of a hippopotamus. He pointed out several shiny scars.

"A lion did that when I tried to take away her prey," he said. "The hospital wasn't any use to me then, and it won't be now."

What good could I be in a case like this? We carried the boy to the fireside. His clothes were soaked with African medicine and he was cold; perhaps we could make him sweat. I held his body, limp now for a moment, as his breath pushed away and pushed away. I tried to give him a little medicine. Mbimbi stood over me, his eyes fixed on the boy, showing all the love Ndembu fathers feel for their sons, who can never inherit from them.

While I looked sadly up at Mbimbi, the body tensed in an awful lock. My thoughts raced frantically. Then the great effort reached a climax, followed by an implosion—a world implosion—a sucking away into another dimension. There was a complete giving away, then a full stop. I went cold and looked down.

Tears rose at once to my eyes. Mbimbi swayed above me like a radio mast in a storm, spurting tears. The village fell into a stunned silence. Then, almost immediately, came the wails, wet flames of helpless sound. Slowly I laid the body down and sat on the log crying bitterly, knowing the grief that was the same for us all.

What about my personal development in the course of these experiences? Could it be said that I was mastering my life? I was living a story in order to tell it, which I am doing in this book. But the reader will find that I've managed to entangle myself into it without being able to get out. A little of myself died with Mbimbi's son; it was my son sick on my lap, my terror when he was dragged from me inwards into another world. Nothing I can do can pull me away from these people into a separate shape that is supposed to be "myself." I fall into each one's life, just as I fell into Vic's life. This isn't the story of a self-directed triumphing individual, but of "someone-plus-a-number-of-particular-people." So you will need to look into the story, into the very rituals to find me, because I have practically disappeared into them. The spirit which has caught me desires to be made manifest, and there's not a thing I can do about it.

Let us return to Kajima.

THE KNIFE

AS TIME TURNED IN Kajima, the condition of the young boys needed attention. For several years now many of them had been growing to adolescence, and somewhere away in the bush they would need a ritual to hold time still, to stop its runaway career, its "shaking." Circumcision would have to be performed, for this would eternalize a certain valued condition—the exposure of the glans during erection—a fleeting experience if the organ were left in its natural state. Circumcision would reveal the desired condition in a permanent form; thus the manhood of the boys could be created, and time could afterwards be released and proceed as before.

A sign of the need was the withdrawn air of Sakeru, the son of Chautongi. It was noticed how he went alone to urinate and seemed depressed. Moreover, certain other friends of his seemed to be in the same condition. Sakeru knew what was the matter. Whenever he had a chance to see the beautifully trimmed penis of his elder brother he was eaten up with envy. Drawing back his foreskin, he gazed with dissatisfaction at his unveiled acorn, still wet, immature, and unreleased from its curtain of flesh. That dirty mucus in the folds was what witches used, to kill a man.

I learned more about this when Manyosa helped her small

grandson to urinate, for while she was watching her lips quivered with a kind of slobbery disgust. "Hanging flesh," she said. "Just like a woman's labia." Her face changed and she grinned up at me as I stood by. "My favorite parts—on me." She pulled out the lips of her mouth; I could see the allusion to the ones she bore on her lower face, as she called it, those grand female lips that she used to love to have stretched by her sweetheart of long ago.

The circumcision ritual was only undertaken every eight years. The growing number of complaints throughout the neighborhood suggested that the time had come around again; so the villagers pulled themselves together to face what was involved in mounting this great rite of passage. Travelers were dispatched down the bush paths carrying messages, information, and plans. The matter duly came to the attention of the court of Kanongesha the chief, and a date was fixed.

Shortly afterwards, Sakeru set out on the trail to the village of Nyaluhana the circumciser, situated beyond the confluence of the Kakula and the turbulent Mudyanyama River.

When he arrived, he addressed Nyaluhana with the traditional words: "Old man circumciser, what's the use of you, you good-for-nothing ham-handed old fool with the blunt knife? They'd never think of holding circumcision here!"

The old man nodded. He fully understood the meaning of this insolent greeting. It was inverted speech, the right way to open the ritual; from now on the participants would be in a different world, an upside-down world, in a time that was no time, a place that was no place. The curve of life would no longer rise on an even graph but would bend over backwards before proceeding, as in all situations of sudden change. They would find themselves upside down, in unexpected situations. Put another way, they were going to exist in a strange pod between one overlapping sphere of life and another, where anything might happen.

Solemnly Nyaluhana marked Sakeru beside the eyes with white clay, the sign of blessing. "Your new name is Warleader," he said. "You shall be the leader of the circumcision boys."

When Vic heard the news he was determined to be present. There was no road to Nyaluhana Village, so he planned to make the fourteen-mile trip on foot, with Musona as guide. I was still weak from my recent bout with malaria, but I decided to join him, at least for the dance of the mothers that was held on the night before the ceremony. We set out early, carrying bread, butter, melon marmalade, and a camera. Rene came along, and Musona took his son Jerry, a six–year–old with gentle popping eyes like those of Manyosa. He trotted along behind Musona, occasionally cocking a cheeky thumb at strangers along the path. Musona walked fast, his thin shoulders and long legs working vigorously.

Our path took us between two rivers along an upland of cassava fields. At length we descended toward the deep and hungry Mudyanyama. The tiny footpath broached the river at an unlikely point and offered as a means of crossing not a bridge, but a tangle of driftwood, around which the river stormed in eddies. Feeling lightheaded with hunger and the recent shock of fever, I lifted my legs easily over the difficult branches, reaching the far shore in a rush, giddy and almost laughing. When all of us had crossed we moved on at the same merciless pace as before. Little Rene grew tired, and we took turns carrying her on our shoulders. Jerry trotted in front with the boundless energy that always surprised me among the Ndembu when I considered the inadequacy of their diet.

The string of hamlets thickened as we drew nearer. We paused at a large village surrounded by mango trees before passing on.

"That was Nyaluhana," said Vic, who had been talking to Musona.

"Oh. Why didn't we stop?"

"You'll see."

We threaded down a short trail, came out into a clearing, and it was as if theater curtains had been drawn aside. A large crowd of people came into view, clustered in groups, gesticulating, making fires, stirring cassava. As soon as they saw us they crowded around for Vic's cigarettes. I edged to one side, found a log to sit on, and stared. So this was the place called the Sacred Fire of Circumcision, the supply camp for the boys in seclusion. I could see the boys crowding the near entrance of the clearing. Through them was pushing an old man who wore a large sun helmet, under which could be seen two hooded sheep-like eyes in a withdrawn black face. His waistcloth drooped down to his feet, so that he appeared to walk without moving any part of his body. This was Master Nyaluhana, the oldest of the circumcisers, whose hand was said to be shaky. I greeted him, but didn't look into his eyes; then I retired again and collapsed on my log.

Meanwhile, the smaller boys clustered around their fathers and tried to straighten their backs. Some were barely five years old. Each boy wore discs of white coloring by his eyes, the blessed mpemba that strengthens the will. Their young faces wore supercilious expressions, though the eyelids twitched. Maybe they judged it better to be present than absent, though the older ones like Sakeru knew very well what was going to happen to them.

Evening was coming down in the enclosed space; people bustled here and there, making rough shelters, tending fires. Women would be needed in this area all through the period of seclusion and healing to cook for their boys, even though they were not allowed in the lodge. Mothers gazed long at their boys, then jerked away and feigned disinterest. I wandered between them toward the far end of the clearing, where I came upon a tall forked pole—a prayer pole—by which stood a mortar. Here the circumcisers assembled to wash themselves with the strengthening astringent liquid in the wooden vase. They were quiet. All around them rose a din from the beer parties that were beginning near the fires. Between the circumcisers and the group of boys, in the very middle of the clearing, grew a wiry thorn tree, the spiny strychnine, with a scar showing where the medicines for the astringent lotion had been taken from the bark. The Ndembu called it "The-Tree-of-Strength-that-the-Elephant-Fails-to-Break."

Now the circumcisers closed around the pole, pouring beer onto the ground for the ancestors. Nyaluhana croaked, "Ancient ancestors, Nyaluhana my ancient mother, chieftainess of long ago, guard my boys when their wounds are open; heal them, my ancestors. May the morning star rise over them when they are healed, as it rose eight years ago."

It was eight years before that the band of circumcisers had collected the most sacred of the medicines, Nfunda, to be used this year for the boys. Nfunda was a black complex powder made from certain ashes and kept in black gourds shaped like bottles. The medicine contained the burnt foreskins of the boys of eight years ago, mixed with those of the boys of sixteen years ago, and so on back to the dawn of Africa. This year it was to be reinforced with a new supply of ashes from the present candidates; and thus these children would be ritually included in the comity of Ndembu men, past and future.

There was a bustle of excitement, for the old men had gone to prepare. The thunder of drums arose, singing broke out, and each boy was swung upon the shoulder of the man who was to guard him in the lodge of healing. Then they whirled around the Tree of Strength, and outside them whirled the mothers. The drums beat louder, and into the circle ran the three circumcisers, each wearing red paint, with a red feather set upright in his hair in front. This was the feather of the lourie, the feather of war and of kings. Each circumciser held high a striped basket, out of which projected two arrows placed there to guard the basket that hid the black bottles of Nfunda.

Now the song ran in an ancient riddle:

You dare not meet the lion,
He'll devour you on the trail
—*Kwalamo!*

You dare not turn in bed,
On your back you'll watch the sky
—*Kwalamo!*

The swamp-bound stork lies low,
Sharp reeds surround her nest
—*Kwalamo!*

And the high-flying kite has stooped
To lay her eggs with the stork
—*Kwalamo!*

The timid lizard turns round,
Lays eggs in the mamba's hole
—*Kwalamo!*

The mother of the child
Long since has cursed my name
—*Kwalamo!*

Mother, keep out and wail,
Your child is taken from you
—*Kwalamo!*

In the lodge beyond the world
The prince and slave are one
—*Kwalamo!*

"Kwalamo!" the voices rolled in deep song. The dreadful sur-
geons crouched and prowled around the thorn like lions, with
their legs wide apart like those of the exposed boys. Out of their
throats came a gargling sound, with slavering and growling. In
the presence of the striped baskets with their fierce arrows, the
little boys climbed yet higher on their guardians' backs, and the
rest ran to the trees to climb up away from the ground lest such
stuff of death should strike them down to the earth, the place
of the dead. But the three circumcisers veered off from the circle
and disappeared.

All through the night the people sang, keeping their fires burning. Every now and then the circumcisers made a new rush upon the camp, and were whirled into the dance around the tree. The sleepy little boys would find themselves on shoulders jigging in the midst of a tempestuous throng. Waking before our fire, we saw two circumcisers face each other, as the drums battered the ears. We saw their indrawn stomachs curving, twitching, and suggesting, the legs gradually bending low, separating, exposing the place where the strong fruits of man lay concealed. We heard their voices, hideous and hoarse, saw their eyes frowning with the intensity of delight, saw in their hands the ancient magic vessels which they turned this way and that, so that the projecting arrows wove figure eights in the air before them.

"Kwalamo!" At the final threatening cry, they sprang erect, lions at the kill. Down again in the crouch of menace, then the lion's spring, the penis leap: death, strength, and sex.

Throughout the night, in devotion to their calling, the circumcisers did not drink, nor did the parents make love. The novices were unnaturally obedient; waking suddenly in the early morning light, they knew what was to come. The mothers withdrew, leaving the children in a little crowd. Sakeru stood amongst them and forced himself to face the camp, impassive and rigid.

Beyond the camp came the sudden din of drums, and down the path ran a spotted figure, which circled toward the children. The women cried out, "The hyena, the hyena!" Then began the Ndembu death-wail, up and down. I clutched Rene's hand and cried, too.

The children were herded toward the path at the far end. Drawn as if to a magnet the mothers followed, their shoulders hunched and hands beside their eyes, seeking the face of a son who looked back with a glittering eye. Halfway up the path they reached a gateway, a bar entry, before which stood the drummers. Mothers and sons jostled in confusion, anxious to postpone the parting, finally circling in a passionate dance. I glanced at the gateway: the top bar was high, like a ranch entrance. There was a crashing from beyond, and I backed away none too soon, for down the path toward us tore a throng of elders and guardians, and in an instant the children's clothes were stripped from them and flung over the top of the bar. Then the spotted hyena came hunting in and out, driving the mothers off, back, back to the clearing, while the whole company of males was borne at great speed through the gate and up into the forest. Nothing remained but a host of little boys' clothes hung over the crossbar—pathetic old ragged bermudas, an ancient cowboy shirt with the check all torn, odd little yellowed shifts, all the foolishness of boys' discarded lives. They were still part of their old lives, so that it would be dangerous for the clothes to touch the ground, the place of blood and death.

I sadly retraced my steps and stood with my women friends as they made their funeral music. Shortly afterwards I set off for home with Rene, for no women were allowed to go beyond the gate into the place of circumcision.

Vic waited with the circumcisers in a clearing in the wilds. He described to me later the careful bearing of the elders, the male comradeship in the lodge. He must have spread his own easiness around him, for nobody minded him being white. They used to kid him: "You make too proud, you still have a white face." It was true. Everyone felt that his great empathy must surely make his face black so that he could be theirs for good. Instead he was to give the world of learning a brilliant analysis of circumcision, from which I have taken my tale.

All was ready in the clearing. For the operation site Nyaluhana had chosen a milk tree, whose leaves exude a white sap. It stood in its dark shiny leaves, representing continuity and nourishment. In its branches hung the basket of black bottles with their promise from the past, and under it were spread the beds of the death-place, the beds of suffering made of forest leaves. Just beyond glimmered the white top of a planted stump of a tear tree, consecrated to the ancestors. The bleeding place was ready, with its long log of blood wood, from the hacked ends of which oozed red coagulating gum. Beside the milk tree stood old man Nyaluhana, wearing only an apron, his chest withered inwards to the ribs, his eyes baleful with power. On each side of his eyes flamed discs of red, and his hand held the knife that he had whetted until he could smell the thin acid steel. The circumcisers were ready.

Into the clearing poured the crowd of victims, hustled by the men. Sakeru the Warleader came first; he was lifted off his feet by two men, his black naked body spread–eagled by their strong arms.

"To the other circumciser, please," he begged. He feared the shaky hand.

The old man heard him and glared.

"To me, Nyaluhana," he croaked, waving him over with his knife. The men laid him down on the death-place; they wrenched his legs apart and held tight. His penis lay open. It gave a little jerk.

Nyaluhana bent over. The drums bellowed and shouting arose to drown out the feared cries of pain. But Sakeru was quiet.

Carefully Nyaluhana put his hand under the timid object, then pulled out the black sleeve that hid the acorn. He loved to free its beauty. His knife pricked one mark; did the body tense a fraction? Then another at the back. That was the line, all around. The old man squinted. Where the first spot of blood welled he tenderly widened the slit with the point of his knife— with the men and Sakeru himself holding absolutely still, anxious that it should be successful—and then took the slit right around the sleeve and drew the sleeve off, leaving a ring of white that immediately turned red. Sakeru in his stark pain was lifted up, raised like a spirit over the ancestor tree, and then set down on his feet. Panting, he straddled toward the bleeding place and seated himself on the log, clearing the mist from his eyes. He was circumcised. Circumcised! A man! It was an irreversible process and he would never again be a child. It was beautiful. In a hoarse, tear-filled voice Sakeru growled "Kwalamo!"

Space on the log soon filled. Next to Sakeru sat a bawling child, swaying in his misery, his father's arms around his shoulders, his wooly head buried in the shirt of the tender friend of all his life. Sakeru's head went back. He carefully held his penis out to bleed into the anthill cup provided in front of him, where the ooze combined with the seethe of ants. What came from the penis would be alive. Sakeru's father stood behind him, aware that this was indeed the warrior. The father's face bore the awesome blankness of the Ndembu in deep emotion.

Much confusion, much careful action were in evidence around them. Soon, amid the blanket of sound, the work was done. Nyaluhana possessed a pot full of black wrinkled pieces, the ingredients for his new Nfunda medicine. A guardian went down the row of boys and sprinkled them with thorn tree medicine, astringent and strengthening. It stung the cuts, but the blood retreated and the flesh drew together. Sakeru's life was now going to be carried on in nakedness, with the open form of his phallus revealed and its graceful arrowhead of love ever before him. He would be exposed to the wilds for three months before he returned home.

Food arrived in the clearing. With wails continually on their lips, the women had been cooking a large meal of cassava and beans, and the scent of the food and the sound of a sizzling calabash of beer roused the boys. Each father rushed for the basket, grabbing rudely, and took food to his own son. Sakeru, as Warleader, had the honor of being fed from the point of Nyaluhana's knife, which was loaded with three balls of cassava. He ate humbly, without using his hands. In a remote corner of his mind reserved for the future, Sakeru was seeing his own son sitting on that log, while he the father, unable to express in words what he felt, fed the honorable boy with the circumcision knife. His eyes glittered and again his head went back.

In camp, the boys settled down to a new life. The guardians piled brushwood around to make a long oval enclosure for the boys at night. This was the lodge, called "The Elephant." There they slept naked on their backs, troubled at first by their wounds and by the cold of the dry season. The men set up a brushwood barrier to hide them from the gate through which they had come, a way they must never pass again, for circumcision is irreversible. Inside the fence extended a long fire, along which they sat and sang at night, all the boys ranged on one side and the elders on the other. They learned archaic words for familiar things: food had a different name and it was rolled in balls like testicles and not sent in on a plate. The boys shuffled carefully toward the table, always holding their legs wide. They were fed well. Whenever they heard the poles pounding meal in the distant camp of the women, the boys shouted "Kwalamo!" and far away high voices replied "Woho!"

One by one the wounds healed. Soon bands of boys set off hunting, coming back with cane rats, coneys, and birds. All spotted things were taboo, all sweet and salt things, for that was the taste of blood and semen. All penises must be quiet now, and a time of peace and friendship followed, both in the lodge and at the women's fires.

Once a strange grunting noise emanated from the sleeping enclosure. Vic, who was in conversation with the circumcisers, went to have a look. A guardian was standing in the lodge, whirling something on a string around his head. Vic gazed at the sight with awe. It was the bullroarer, the same soundmaker that the Australian aborigines used in their initiation, and also the Bororo of Brazil.

"In every circumcision lodge we whirl the Lion of Ancient

Times," the youth insisted. "The women hear," he grinned, "and run in panic. And they may well run, for a monster is coming."

Vic fingered the thing, a heavy piece of blood wood carved into the shape of a fish, with a hole to take the string. As it whirled, the sharp edge caught the air and turned it back and forth, producing the deep sound Vic had heard.

When the boys' wounds had almost healed, the monster came. Sakeru, always on the lookout, happened to turn, and saw passing behind him a tall striped creature with an enormous head. He gasped and all the boys gathered to look. The thing groveled along the hedge, the drums beat loud. Where had it come from? Out of the ground? It lolloped and swayed and showed its great hands, bound around with knotted root fiber. Then it took a stick and advanced upon the boys, knees bent, rattles clacking on its calves, head held back in a majestic sun-ward gaze. From the back of its head rose a threefold serpent, thrusting its tail back and over and up until it stood on end, while the sun that was blazoned over the brow faced up to the sun in the sky. Lightning lines lay across the brow, creating a frown in a jagged row; and tears came from the eyes, long tears. It was mourning for itself, with its little square mouth shaped ready to utter—but no sound came. As the creature drew nearer, the boys ran off squealing. It floundered at them and danced by to the singing of the elders. As it went a blow was suddenly felt on each back. Now the glade was full of crying, while the sorrowful figure wallowed in the center, seemingly hardly able to stand.

The drums rolled out their rhythms, irresistibly calling. The thing revived and seemed to scoop up energy with its hand. The boys could only guess what the creature—huge, ancestor-given, and bearded—meant. All their old fears of the night, fears of helpless hypnotically-moving dying men, rose up in them. The elders knew it as Chizaluki, the Mad Chief, uniting the mindlessness of death with the enigma of the soul's immortality. Sakeru didn't fear it, he loved it, the dying lord that yearned toward the sun: it had blessed him with a beating.

Not long before the end of seclusion, another bizarre figure strolled around the lodge. This was a tall woman with a heavy crude face wearing a headcloth, a blouse, and a skirt, below which ugly muscular legs could be seen. The boys looked down at the legs and laughed. It was the Nyakayowa, the Ancient Mother.

"You're to be married, you 'first wives'," declared the guardians. "There's your husband."

The little boys held their heads, dizzy with the puzzle of it. Yes, as novices they were called first wives, but how could this woman be a husband? To prepare for what followed, each guardian fed his boy with the oily meat of tortoises so that the "head" of his penis would come out, long and enquiring. Then each guardian led his boy up to the Nyakayowa, who was now sitting entirely covered by a blanket with legs outspread.

"Eh! Eh!" said the child in horrified glee. Through a hole in the blanket he saw a black swelling.

"Go on, touch her, touch her."

The child felt his own strong heat then, his own swelling, and without looking at his guardian he wriggled closer and closer to Nyakayowa and finally laid his tool against hers.

"You are a man," said the guardian, grinning cheerfully. "Take some Nfunda now." The guardian had the black bottle open, and proffered some of the black substance on the end of the circumciser's knife. The boy ate solemnly.

"We give you back your bodies," came the statement.

Now the taboos fell from them, one by one. They feasted on salted cassava and they spotted themselves all over with white clay dots. Their lithe bodies jumped about like harlequins. They were caught and given grass skirts.

"Come on, wives," mocked the guardians. "We're off to scare the life out of your mothers."

While they were busy dressing, a scandal was uncovered. One of the boys had been given a pair of bermudas by his guardian, and was wearing them under his skirt.

"Heh!" growled Nyaluhana when he saw the pants. "Take off that garbage! This isn't a missionary meeting. Pants at the dance of the spotted boys? Impossible!" Nyaluhana turned and left, furious—the Ndembu fundamoka exit.

"Pants, is it?" yelled Nyaluhana's nephew.

"These grass things aren't decent," complained the guardian, who had had a year of mission schooling. "They're going to meet their mothers."

"Don't talk like the Europeans here!" said the other. They grabbed at each other and fell to the ground in an angry tussle. Sakeru watched. He wasn't worried about his mother. He was now a man, a full member of the Nyachintanga lineage.

The drums were thundering, for the mothers awaited them at the women's clearing. Quickly the offending boy was stripped of his bermudas and they all lined up. Each guardian chose a boy that wasn't his own and lifted the child on his shoulder.

"The return! The return!" They ran full tilt down through the forest into the open, into the public world that the boys had not seen for three months.

"Yey, yey, yey!" shrieked the women in joy. The boys were carried around the center thorn in a streak of black and white spots, each boy clacking a pair of sticks behind his head. The mothers ran around in an outer circle looking for their sons.

"There's his guardian, I see his guardian. But he's carrying someone else! Where's my son? He must be dead. Yey, yey! They've killed him. Eh! Why, there he is, Sakeru, Sakeru!"

"Warleader now, mother," called down Sakeru from his height.

Another voice cried, "That one must be mine. No, who's he? Ah, there you are, Sakwimba!"

And another—"Mukengi!"

"Mother!"

They were all present, safe and sound.

After the parents and children were sorted out, the great celebration with feasting and dancing began. All Mwinilunga District seemed to be there to help drink the thirty-six calabashes of beer that had been assembled. Tirelessly they danced around the thorn, charged up with joy and relief.

Toward dawn Sakeru looked around sleepily at the scene: the glow of the fires, the still shuffling dancers, and the brightening sky. There in the east . . .

"The star!" he called. "The star is rising!" Over the treetops Venus shone, a pinprick of dazzling light.

It was the star of beginnings, the beginning of the day and of adulthood, the star of the revelation of the glans. At every circumcision it was seen like this, and the old men's faith in its coming had never been betrayed.

At Sakeru's first call the men rushed toward the lodge. Now a roar was heard, and another light rose furiously.

"The lodge is burning, kwocha, kwocha!" cried the women. "Hide yourselves, boys, hide your eyes, or you'll go mad."

Suddenly Sakeru's memory came back to him, of the first touch of the knife. No, he could never look back. There was a blanket on top of him now, and a mat descended on top of that, and his mother was beating at the mat, crying, "Hide, hide," while he stuffed his mouth with the blanket, pushed it into his eyes, pounded and worked his hands, squeezed tight his eyes. "Away, away from the past, into the future." Then he could breathe more freely. The banging ceased, the roar lessened. He had come out the other side. He pushed the blanket away and stood up, finding his guardian waiting for him.

"Up on my shoulder."

The guardians bore all the spotted company down to the river, where they dumped them in the water. The grass skirts floated off and the spots were washed away with the uncleanness of childhood. Cheerfully they scrambled out to occupy themselves with the task of dressing up, including hair trimming, oiling, and an entire set of new clothes to put on. Each boy was adorned with a band of beads around the hair line and over the top—a mess of little boys full of glee and fooling around.

Meanwhile, the circumcisers were taking an indispensable task in hand. Now that the lodge was burnt they needed to link this initiation with the last one and forge the link to the future one, eight years hence. Ndembu men had no male lineage like the female lineage; the continuity of their brotherhood lay solely in those black bottles, enclosed in baskets and guarded by arrows. The bottles must never touch the ground, for that would mean death and the severing of continuity with ages past.

Nyaluhana solemnly approached the place of circumcision, the death-place, passing on to join his men in the ashes of the burnt-down lodge. The men brought a red cock and laid it at his feet. Sitting in the place of the past, with a broken pot before him, he took the cock, made a prayer to the ancestors, and cut off its head as it struggled. Then he held the body neck downwards, so that the blood dripped into the pot. Blood was the first substance of power, and the broken pot represented death. Nyaluhana then mixed in the black Nfunda powder from his bottles. Around the men lay the ashes from the home of the boys' suffering, some of which they gathered up and added to the pot. They stirred the mixture with the stick that Chizaluki had used to beat the boys. The old bedding from under the milk tree, black with blood, provided more ashes, with some particles of the blood log, the tear tree, and the mothers' cooking fire. The men added sacred white beer, some of which was poured on the ground for the spirits of the dead. Lastly, Nyaluhana drew to him another broken pot, holding a lumpy black dust, the foreskins of the boys, which he had reduced to ashes on the fire and thus preserved. He added ritual oil to this powder and carefully emptied the black fluid into his ash mixture. Again he stirred.

Then two guardians were summoned and made to strip completely.

"Sit there," said Nyaluhana, pointing to the ashes of the lodge. "Face each other now, nearer, nearer." At his direction one placed his legs over the other's legs, and they drew closer still, whirling their stomachs while the elders sang. The one with the legs uppermost lifted his penis and tied it up against his belly with a string. Man and "woman" waited. Nyaluhana then placed his pot of Nfunda in the space between their legs. Holding the sacrificed cock's body, he cut it open and carefully drew out the viscera and reproductive organs. Then, holding them firm, he squeezed until both semen and waste fell into the ash mixture in the pot. The intestines he stretched into a rope to bind the couple together, winding it around the testicles and penis of the man and leading it across to the testicles of the "woman."

"Do not break it," commanded the old man. "Now do your part."

Again their stomachs began to contract, while they kept their eyes on the communicating viscera and the pot of the future between them. The lips of the man began to move. Then it came, a surge from his penis which spurted into the pot before him.

Suddenly Nyaluhana's knife flashed between them, drawing gently across one man's penis and the other's testicles without harming them. Nyaluhana removed the objects and up sprang the men, for the elders were immediately after them with sticks, forcing them to hop over the red-hot ashes until they halted on the very bed where Warleader had suffered. There the two men received a beating, thus reversing time from the moment of genital power to childhood. The two struggled to a dry tree without bark and kicked it; the "circumcised" tree was their sanctuary.

Nfunda was complete. Nyaluhana filled his bottles, stoppered them, and carefully replaced them in the basket.

Chief Kanongesha has arrived at the thorn tree. The boys, dressed in their finery, are carried by the guardians into the clearing amid hoots of triumph. A long mat is unrolled, and the boys are set down on it. The chief sits before the thorn tree on a carved stool, wearing a white and black bead crown with many projecting horns, and around his waist a leopard skin apron. The drums and the royal xylophone begin their unsteady rhythm. Sakeru the Warleader dances up to the chief and strikes the chief's short sword with his knife. He straddles, advances, and retreats in his dance, elbowing and pawing with his feet like the bull buffalo, the strongest animal in Africa. Then each boy follows with a dance of his own.

Finally Warleader approaches the chief himself, and speaks in his deepening voice.

"I am a man! You, chief, are a fool and a rogue, nothing but garbage. Hah! I, Warleader, command you, chief. Have better manners, do not be so greedy, feed your children."

Kanongesha's face is impassive. He observes the strength of the boy and his defiance. It is right.

"Sire," says the senior guardian. "We have guarded the children well; count them, not one of them is missing." And it is done.

The chief makes a sign; payments are handed over and the feasting begins.

THRESHOLD

THOSE BOYS WERE HARDY. While they were living naked in the lodge July had arrived, and the cold was intense. We ourselves did not find it too pleasant living in a thin umbrella tent; I could hardly stand the flapping canvas any longer. Here in the uplands, although we were just south of the equator, Vic found slivers of ice on the windshield of the truck, which reminded him he had to arrange for sturdier housing. He met with Kajima and his men to discuss a replacement for the tent. At first everyone fantasized about a large brick house; all argued that we should settle down and become farmers. It would cost us £200. We were aghast. We could never find that much money on a graduate student's grant. In the end Vic settled to have temporary grass huts erected for £20 on a site as near to the village as possible.

Freddy and I wandered around the periphery of Kajima among middens and yellow scrub, and out to the trees where the bush began. Freddy was just as adventurous and enthusiastic as I was. We were pioneers seeking a place for our homestead. Rejecting one site after another, we came upon two trees that had been left to grow when the land had been a cassava field some years back. Suddenly, home was written all over this spot. We walked around the nearest tree, touching the trunk with kindly fingers. The stretches of grass and young bush between the two trees came into focus as a campground; this might actually be our home. To try it out I sat down under the tree and thought vaguely of a picnic at first; then as the westering sun lingered on the spot, I was loath to desert it. It was ours and would be lonely without even a plan made. We got up, checked directions, and began to map out the camp.

"Here'll be the kitchen, here'll be the living hut."

"Here'll be my hut," said Freddy, sitting down on the place he had chosen.

"The other tree can shade the living hut. Look, its door would face Kajima Village."

The nearer tree was shady and had a friendly curve. It would be fine with a lawn around so that people could rest and chat in the shade. The creeping grass that grew there would make the lawn. We showed the site to Vic; we showed it to Master Kajima when he came with Vic to inspect. Then we formally asked the twinkling old man for permission to build on this plot. "I agree, sirs," he replied, but he seemed to be saying "my dears."

When the men had left I saw to my wonder that our new path to the village was already made. Freddy and I, and Vic and Kajima, had by our coming and going trodden down the path that was to become everybody's highway. So many times in this country we were to feel "the hand of emotion lightly strike across the chords of our hearts," a phrase that I considered not sentimental, but an almost clinical description of the feeling. That hand was powerfully, intimately in contact with certain vibrating chords inside, very like the fibrils of the ear or the cords of the voice. And why the sound was sweet was a long story, concerned with two ancient traditions—ours in the reading of poetry, the Ndembu's in the poetic range of their symbols. We knew we were lucky to come to this land, for if we had never left home we would have become bitter and cynical, like so many in that disappointed society. I asked myself who cares about the polished doorstep of a rented house? But I found myself caring about this neglected stretch of bush, which with a

little help I could turn into a cozy home. Rilke said it before, in
the "Ninth Duino Elegy":

> Threshold: how much it can mean
> to a pair of lovers, that they should be wearing their own
> worn threshold a little, they too, after the many before,
> before the many to come, . . . as a matter of course!
> *Here* is the time for the Tellable, *here* is its home.
> Speak and proclaim. More than ever
> the things we can live with are falling away, and their place
> being oustingly taken up by an imageless act. . . .
> Praise this world to the Angel, not the untellable. . . . show him
> some simple thing, remoulded by age after age,
> till it lives in our hands and eyes as a part of ourselves.
> Tell him *things*.

Very soon four round grass huts stood in an oval ring: it was
a little village, with the larger tree dominating the far end and
the grass kitchen hut at the end nearest Kajima. The huts all
faced inward, with small paths connecting them. The space between them had been cleared of stumps and the lawn was beginning. The path from the door of the living hut passed by the
shade tree, then by the kitchen, before proceeding into Kajima
ten yards beyond.

At the other end of the encampment a discreet path led to the
latrine, where a grass screen surrounded a deep hole. I provided
the latrine with a seat made of a wooden margarine box, with a
wide oval hole in the top painstakingly sculpted to the right
shape with my own hands. I was proud of my latrine; it was
doubly useful, for the inaccessible depths below the seat proved
a good place to throw stacks of glossy women's magazines sent
to me by white ladies from town, but not my kind of thing at
all, or for the frantic disposal of Marxist literature when government officials paid a visit.

For the living hut, some mats were made of long split canes
from the Lunga riverside. They provided a milk-yellow floor,

ridgy and naturally polished. A local carpenter produced a large roughly-fashioned cupboard made of the blood wood, a kind of teak. It was paneled, and glowed deeply when I rubbed it with brown shoe polish. A rough Windsor chair and loveseat also were fashioned from blood wood, with thongs across the seats. I cushioned the seats with brilliant orange and green calico from the district store, stuffing the cushions with grass from the bush. Beside the grass wall stood a bookcase of red planks, filled with the family's library—children's classics, anthropology, murder mysteries, and poetry. A wonderfully neat filing cabinet was made to measure by the Ndembu carpenter from forest timber; this stood beside the door. There were two windows. The glass and the tacks that secured the glass were the only construction materials in the hut that had been brought from town; even the window frames were tied into place with root string through gaps left in the straw walls. Root and bark string held the whole hut together. Then there were the two camp cots we had brought with us, set close together and spread with a brilliant green and red coverlet made from store cloth printed all over with pictures of African huts.

On the night the hut was finished, I put on my sky blue dress with a design of white arabesques, while Vic took a book and sat on the loveseat. His dark hair stood out richly against the orange curtains behind. I lay on the bed reading, pausing once in a while to look around.

"I think it's a beautiful little hut," I said.

Vic looked up. "It's all I ever want."

A few weeks after the hut had been completed, the local white rancher paid us a visit. He wore expensive safari clothes and highly polished shoes, which made us immediately aware of our own graying garb. He arrived with a pale-eyed underling, his labor manager, and on entering looked around as if there were nowhere to sit. The tall rancher was used to giving orders, it was obvious; the world he came from was not our now-familiar world of manners, but one of power. He had hooded eyes and a mouth that looked guilty because it looked for guilt in others. He finally sat down, his whole being suggesting his weary disapproval of these anthropologists. The cookies I had especially baked—my best orange teacakes—were completely forgotten. Did they drink tea? No, they refused tea.

We made conventional politenesses. What had the rancher come to say?

"You're going native, I hear," he finally bit out. "It makes it very difficult for us to keep the respect of the natives. The example, you know." He had a South African accent.

He looked upward at the thatch. "You've not been long in this country, I can see. You've made a bad start; it's illegal to house children in a grass camp like this, you know."

We muttered something, our faces controlled.

"There was a case the other day," he cut in. "People"—he meant whites, of course, because the Africans weren't people to him—"insisted on living in grass huts. The children were inside, and whoosh! The hut caught fire. Those children were *fried*." His eyes glittered queerly.

Then he became casual. "Absolutely no hope, of course. . . . The smell!" We sat transfixed.

He pointed upward. "See the cone shape? Acts like a funnel, crowns in a second." He stood up carefully, as if he might bump his head.

Somehow the visit came to a polite end. No one watched the smart Landrover leave. Vic walked to and fro, frowning terribly and biting his knuckles; he had been weighing the glory of a fight against his opportunity to do fieldwork.

I looked around the camp where straw from the building still lay strewn about, mingled with dead leaves. I kicked it; it looked dusty. I had left it there to keep down the dust swamps that had developed below the dead grass, churned into existence by many passing feet, weak areas that had worked deep into the friable soil, not yet hardened by rain.

Inside the huts the mosquito nets were dirty, and the matting showed wear. My face in the mirror was reddish with enlarged pores. My nose looked more bulbous than usual, and very shiny. I pulled out a lock of hair; it was stringy, greasy. Nevertheless I tried a smile, but it came out as a wolfish grin. No, there it was, a really warm smile. I could still look handsome, I told myself, moving into a glamorous three-quarter position, and to prove it I brushed my hair and pinned it up. "Always after the event," I sighed.

The Africans filtered back into the clearing, and I forgot to decide whether the visitor ought to be taken seriously. The next day, however, I swept out the entire encampment and filled up one whole garbage pit with strawy muck. The soil beneath the straw had consolidated somewhat and gave us no more trouble.

The whites' move had been designed to get rid of us; with good instinct they regarded our ideas as communistic and knew we were undermining the distinction between white and black, boss and worker. It was Vic's obstinacy and my optimism that rendered us immune, the result being that neither of us got cold feet. Gradually our increasing involvement with the villagers, in comradeship and the sharing of medicines, made it impossible for the whites to make any further moves against us.

Long after I had forgotten the rancher, we had our fire. The story was told in the Ndembu villages, and also back home in many a pub where returning anthropologists met, adding to their repertoire of snake stories, epics of the giraffe hunt, tragedies of lost fieldnotes, crocodile fights. The story told how it was Rene's birthday, how Musona entered the kitchen to turn the joint roasting in the dutch oven and somehow spilt all the fat into the flames; how at the resulting majestic column of fire he bundled Freddy out of the hut—the grass roof had caught!—how the frightful roar precipitated the whole population of greater Kajima out of their huts; how Musona amid a crowd of his friends advanced and pulled the water drum away from the side of the burning hut so that firefighters could obtain water; how Vic and I flung bowlful after bowlful at the flames. And all the while behind us stood an awe-inspiring figure, Chizaluki, the Crazed Chief himself, still making the rounds from Nyaluhana to dance at Kajima. Heads turned as he moved among the onlookers with his gibbering motions, horrifying and horrified.

I looked up from him to the fire. The forest was aflame.

"It's going for the latrine!" I shouted. It was too late: the latrine went up like a torch. The village audience stood openmouthed, admiring the sight. Suddenly I remembered.

"My seat, my beautiful seat!" I started forward. Then Vic caught sight of a worse danger: flames reached for his gasoline supply, kept in a drum that stood upright among the grasses. The fire advanced almost playfully, painting the grasses a bright orange before leaving them curled up in blackness. Stop it! But how? Vic set a line of men with branches of green leaves to beat out the flames; I joined them in my sandals. Meanwhile, I could hear Vic behind me, busy with the drum. He screwed the cap on tight, then rocked the four–hundred–pound container until it fell over on its side, and trundled it away into the middle of Kajima, where he got himself under one end and heaved it upright again. Everyone breathed a sigh of relief.

It was late afternoon before the fire was out and all was quiet in the bush. I turned toward the familiar path to the latrine, for my bladder was tense. The path was blackened; I had forgotten, there was no latrine. But what was that whitish object standing among the scorched tree trunks? I approached, avoiding red-hot cinders. It was my beloved seat, still in place, with the cans of Lysol and insecticide still there, as were three charred science fiction magazines, reminders of many happy times of peace. We merely needed a new screen, and life could go on. Hurriedly, not looking around, I used the seat and returned.

The kitchen had disappeared, leaving a kind of altar of mud bricks that still supported the dutch oven. Musona stepped in on his bare soles, opened the lid, and seized the joint; it was perfectly cooked, thus illustrating the Chinese story about the fool who burnt down his house to cook a pig.

Everyone had forgotten about Rene's birthday. We found she had been crying for a long time: "My birfday's a' gone."

"Look what I've got for you," I said, taking from the dining hut a small birthday cake I had put away earlier.

"Ooh," said Rene, and poked a finger into it. Her ash-stained face looked up smiling.

THE MILK TREE

IT WAS THROUGH RENE that I first became familiar with the girls' initiation ceremony. Kandaleya, Manyosa's elder daughter, was teaching Rene the heel-drumming dance that the initiate performs at the climax of the rites. Eventually, I had a chance to join in a full ceremonial when Kajima's daughter Mwenda was ready for her puberty rites.

Initiation prepares a girl for her future as a sexually mature woman. It takes her through a stage at which all her feelings are strange; it lifts her, so to speak, across the gap between childhood and womanhood, and in order to do so it uses ritual that works, as myth does, in the realm of the imagination. When I experienced the ritual, much of which had never been recorded, it became clear not only that the women of this society possessed something akin to religious genius, but also that the ritual I was performing—this concretized poetry—was saying something that words could not say, and was achieving a pleasure and social unity that symbolic action alone could encompass.

I managed to get up at 5:30 A.M. and struggle out to Kajima for the dawn rites. Before me spread the sleeping village, the dim ring of huts barely visible, some little and square with thatch that converged to a point, others larger, with a ridge and a jaunty curve to the roof. Above them rose the forest, still in darkness.

I crossed the plaza quietly. Now I saw that the mistress of ceremonies, a black and jovial woman, aptly called the midwife, was standing outside her hut. It was Mwenda's great-aunt, Natalie; this was her day. "Ey! Yey-yey!" she shouted, and plunged straight into her neighbor's hut. Instantly a bleary-eyed woman emerged—Chautongi, who was Mwenda's cousin. Yana, Mwenda's sister, joined them, making three, all related familiarly through women, so that the mother-lineage was alive in them. Natalie led us at once into the bush to where a milk tree grew, a shrub that bore dark green leaves which exuded a brilliant white sap when broken off. The sap was actually rubber, for the tree was a species of latex. But the sap was also wild milk, the milk of the world of symbols, the sacred milk of a matrilineal people. And now there came toward us, through untrodden bush, from a strange direction, the girl herself, known in initiation as Guinea Fowl, tall and mute, robed in a blanket.

Quickly the women prepared a new fire, and the robed visitor drew near and warmed herself. We began to feel cheerful. Suddenly a circle formed around the milk tree, and in a trice everyone was dancing around. They burst out singing, the real singing, harsh and terrific, clapping an echo from the end of the forest and plunging it out into the plain.

"She has grown up! The baby is woman! My child is ripe!"

The final vibrating harmony ceased and the women looked anxiously around at the forest. There was a lift to the air, brightness was flowing through the trees.

"God will see," they warned each other, and hastened to spread an antelope skin on the ground beneath the dew-raining leaves of the milk tree. I watched, getting in the way, while Natalie went to the fire, lifted Mwenda, and carried her the short distance to the antelope skin. The girl fell limp upon the hide.

The midwife removed the blanket from her naked body and turned her on her side, bending the limbs into a small bundle, just as the Ndembu bury their corpses, but this body was warm, nubile. Up they looked again, fearing a presence.

Natalie turned to the sister. "Give us a blanket, quick!"

Yana opened up a big one and they spread it over the girl, tucking it around her and over her head while she moved sleepily beneath. The blanket enclosed her like a womb. Within it she breathed small air, she was dead, forgotten. Yet she was a warm baby.

"Do not move," spoke the voice of the midwife. The day ahead would be long, and heat, dust, hunger, and thirst were likely to work upon the girl and destroy the humble peace she should feel. But now the command was unnecessary: the girl was asleep. Above her, the dance burst out in all its strength. The day of her death and rebirth had begun.

Light in a vast tunnel speared through the forest. Then for the first time I noticed the milky glow of something poised over the topmost sprays of the sacred bush. I looked closer and saw white beads hung over the top of a stick; no, the stick was an arrow, its long iron point biting into the ground and its shaft fledged with feathers, over which the white beads lay. It was the arrow of the young man who was going to marry Guinea Fowl at the end, and the beads were her future children. Singing, the women passed and passed before the arrow in an endless circling, bending and swaying their hips, then elbowing up to clap at the very moment of syncopation when there was no sound, and immediately the tremendous black rasp of music fell into place again.

The milk-and-gray of the dawn ritual gradually metamorphosed into an orange sunlit scene of jollity. Women arriving from neighboring villages burst into the small circle, each one adding a new stanza to the song and receiving a thunderous chorus line from the crowd. The clearing widened as the stumps at the edge of the blanket were collected and placed under the milk tree. The circle began to encroach on the outer saplings, which Chautongi dealt with, cutting them down to ground level with a slender ax. The dance floor was being made as it was danced upon, just as dancing has always created its halls and bands and customs down the ages.

Gay dresses now appeared in the clearing. An older woman entered dressed in green and gold, a fantastic pattern crisp from the store. She had braided up her hair into three ridges from front to back and had bound them with an olive band. The sun glittered on the complex braids as if they were black diamonds. On her arms were bangles, and her face was adorned with discs of glowing green on the tip of each cheekbone. The smooth everted lips were painted the same raving green; my eyes kept returning to her face as she sashayed before me. Quite jealous, I stood up in my dismal brown dress and found a space in the circle myself. The women smiled and I clapped and swayed, showing off a little.

Men had been standing about in the village, waiting. But it was their time now. The drums moved up and young men leaped daringly into the circle, moving around like clowns, their bold embarrassed faces thrust out at the girls in front. Two or three men provided new energy for the treading wheel of the dance. I moved within its circle, trying the jaunty swing of the hips and the urge of the arms upward to the clap. The beat of the clapping held me until at last I was in rhythm, as my ears and throat and muscles responded to the harmony, to the gritty plaintive beauty of the song, while the drums rocked the ether and ax-irons struck in pairs clapped out their deafening syncopation.

In the middle of the ever-advancing circle two women side-stepped each other continually in the curtsey of Morris dancing; this was the original Moorish dancing. With each step they plunged with a shout and two claps to opposite sides, before reversing positions, all the while smiling ecstatically at each other over an odd pile of cloth that lay under the milk tree, right in the center of the din—Mwenda, wrapped in a blanket.

The sun stood at the zenith. The midwife, wearing a pointed woollen cap, entered the circle and carefully turned Mwenda so that her body faced away from the sunset, toward the dawn. The girl now faced the milk tree, toward her awakening. The dance continued with increasing clamor. A hunter, a tall stern-faced wisecracker, was dancing in the circle. He beat time as if the devil were in him, to which the crowd responded like a row of inspired stamping machines, while the drums belched out explosions of pepper into the air. Women circled around with thrilling eyes, shouting the lewd and graceful lines at the tops of their voices.

> Momma, Momma! The basket is full,
> Heavy, ready—it's killing me,
> —*Ah, come.*

> The hunter's steel struck the flint,
> Out comes a spark in a long point,
> —*Whooh!*

> Drrr! Drrr!
> He's beating the side of my drum with his stick,
> Momma, I cry,
> —*Drrr! Drrr!*

Then a change of tone:

> I'm off, off. Who are you, small man?
> Pooh! Huh! I'm through with you.

Then the reply:

> I know whom you've taken up with now.
> Come back, honey, I want you, I need you,
> —*Yey!*

And they all trilled.

Hooting arose when Mangaleshi danced into the ring displaying a canoe-shaped platter crammed with leaves. She flung them like fate indiscriminately at the women, and they ran and clutched at them. She chortled around the circle, chanting about leaves and children as multitudinous as the forest itself. A tall man broke in, a savage with a long smile. He waved and jeered and lifted up a basket full of chopped-off anthill towers, long and hard, seething with ants—suffused with them, you might say. He heaved the basket erect in salute, while everyone howled in recognition. The dance swirled on.

The crowd reminded me of some great Victorian mural in which small dramas occur all over the canvas. At a slight distance a young woman in red stood beside Nyachitela the witch, trying out what looked like a rotted drum. They were arguing hotly. The lady in red was Evita, Nyachitela's daughter, known to one and all as the Kajima Road Hooker.

"Fetch me water, water!" shouted Evita to young Samawika, who was looking on. "Water for my mpwita!" People were not paying her as much attention as she would have liked. Seeing my gaze, she returned it with a haughty stare.

"White Mishy!" she bellowed. "Come over here. Come on, I'm going to play you my mpwita." Her mpwita appeared to be that old rotted drum. I approached unwillingly, for my head was starting to ache at the sound of Evita's voice. Evita's nose was long and Roman and her eyes popped a little; her back was hunched with willfulness. I was about to turn away.

"This instant!" I froze. The woman was awful.

But my curiosity was hooked by the drum. It was open at one end, and I looked inside. There was something down there, attached to the bottom. At that moment Samawika came through the crowd with a small bowl of water. Evita took it. "You scum," she hissed. "That's not much water for my mpwita!" She wetted her hand and reached inside the drum, taking hold of the object inside. It was a reed, connected with the resonating skin stretched over the lower end. Evita held the reed in her wet hand, and began, horribly, to slide her fingers up and down the

reed: "Ugh, ugh, ugh, ug-urgh, urgh-ug, ug-ugh." Nyachitela
beat the side of the drum with a stick. The noise was syncopated
and curiously obscene. I watched, transfixed. Evita seized my
hand and passed it along the reed. The slightest rub produced
an embarrassingly loud sound. After a moment I withdrew my
hand, feeling simultaneously repelled and satisfied. "I suppose
this goes into my fieldnotes," I thought. "The feeling, though,
what about that? A nasty feeling, when resisted. But hot . . . .
The masturbation drum, you might call it." Years later I discovered that the mpwita had crossed the South Atlantic and is pres-
ently used at the Rio Carnival under the name cuica. It still
makes an emotional sound, though higher in pitch, like the
whimpering of a bitch at the moment of breeding.

"This is the woman's drum," Evita said proudly, and she continued her rubbing and croaking.

Suddenly Nyachitela staggered to her feet; a vain alluring
smile spread across her face as she stood there. After a moment
the crowd broke into laughter, and peering over shoulders I
caught sight of her stomach. She had tucked her dingy blouse
up under her armpits, pulled down her skirt, and with feet
placed wide apart was revolving her stomach like a wheel. All
the women in the crowd clapped, belting out a hot suggestive
ditty about the men down the copper mines. Up and around,
up and around twisted the ancient muscles, like a treacle pudding being stirred. Nyachitela held the ecstasy for a minute.
Then her eyes shot toward me and, tittering a little, she lowered
her blouse. The people sang on, and while they finished the
verse she stood her ground, motionless save for the unmistak-
able rhythm under her blouse. In the midst of the din and the
laughter I looked enquiringly at Evita. "It's the dance on the
bed," she yelled shamelessly. The Ndembu loved this peculiar
contrast between sexiness and old age, rather like a femme fatale
portrayed in drag.

The grunting of the drum continued. As bad luck would have
it, Evita caught sight of Rene in the crowd.

"Come and do the heel drumming, Rene! This instant!" Thrust to and fro in the press, poor little Rene tried to oblige, but then drew toward me. I took her hand and led her out of the village onto the plain where a little stream wandered. Peace.

After a time my curiosity overcame me and I decided to return to the village, but quietly. Sneaking around the kitchen huts with Rene, I came upon Katayi, the mother of the Guinea Fowl, and Natalie the midwife standing over mortars, pounding cassava. Loose white cassava flour lay around in drifts. It was quiet here. Rene went off to play.

The midwife slowly left the mortar and placed the pole against the wall.

"What are you doing," I asked. "Why aren't you at the dance?"

"We're cooking for the feast," she said. She and I sat down together to share a cigarette, while we discussed the next stage. Katayi regarded us uneasily. She kept coming up and going away again.

"Go on, talk, talk," she complained. "It's me who has all the work and no fun."

Natalie, ignoring her, turned to me. "They're about to start building the seclusion hut. While Mwenda is a Guinea Fowl she doesn't live with people. She's set-on-one–side, not an ordinary person. It's a time of change, you'll see." And she would say no more.

In the yard in front of me the ground had already been cleared for the new hut, and a couple of poles stood ready. Two boys strolled through the trees; they swaggered forward and each seized a pole.

"Sixpence for this job!" shouted the younger rudely.

"Huh! Only a penny for you, useless creature!" shrieked Katayi, advancing with both fists waving. The boys stuck to their poles and did not move. I watched, my mouth open.

"It's all right," said Natalie, seeing my face. "Never mind her bad temper, they're always like that. The bigger boy is Makanjila, the bridegroom, and that younger one is his brother, Wankie, the lesser bridegroom. They've come to set up the milk tree pole and blood tree pole and pitch the roof."

The boys still hadn't moved. "These are the stingiest in-laws ever known," said Wankie, and the other nodded. Both women turned savagely and argued with them, goading them on to start building the hut.

I had forgotten there was to be a bridegroom. This whole affair was the preparation for a wedding, as well as the creation of a woman. These people were matrilineal, well–nigh matriarchal. The women helped themselves to everything, they were blazing with life. And they helped themselves to marriage. A girl would run away instantly if she were badly treated. I had seen the women's rightful and magnificent anger in their husbands' huts.

So the female child, the fierce child, flat-chested to begin with but increasingly filled with longing, would rush up to the starting post of life, would fall into adolescence, and, seduced by her own beauty, plunge into dreaming. She would widen and open, her hips would be unbearable to her, she would sink into the hands of her friends, lie under the blanket, transported while in the state of death into the even stranger state of sex, and then, in the seclusion hut, what then? I turned to look. A shaggy object rose from the clearing. I sighed. The boys were still quarreling with Katayi; they had acted quite objectionably, I thought.

Nevertheless, in the end the seclusion hut was tidy enough. It was built like a simple inverted V. Wankie, the lesser bridegroom, climbed atop of it, then carefully stood up straight.

"Whooh!" I said. He grinned down at me. He had business there of some sort. He sat down, settled himself around the pointed roof, and grinned still more comfortably.

"The bridegroom himself would be too embarrassed to sit there, don't you see?" said the midwife, pulling my arm suggestively. Apparently everyone was enjoying the symbolism of the hut. It went like this: inside, the rafters were splayed open, like the bride's legs. Outside, the hut was pointed, like her husband. The little bridegroom held his legs splayed on the point like a woman, but still he was on top of the roof, like a rooster. The bridegroom himself would later be borne within the splayed legs of the bride, and he was the one with the point. He couldn't have enacted the little bridegroom's ambiguous role, that female role. One person, the lesser bridegroom, curiously represented two people. And afterwards, two people would become one. It was enough to make you smile.

The crowd around the milk tree was still thick, but now women were leaving it to gather by the midwife's cooking fire. The midwife worked busily in her shortened skirt. She had already rolled out various sticky wads of cassava pudding onto platters that occupied a large area of ground in the cooking yard. She rapidly rotated each plate, patting the soft stuff into a swelling mound. When she had done, Katayi slowly took from the fire a large aluminum pan, shining gray on the inside and matted black on the outside. It was full of red beans. She tilted the pan to drain off some of the liquid. Then she poured piles of beans onto dishes until there were enough for an army. The women started forward to pick them up.

"Eh!" cautioned the midwife. "Wait, we haven't gotten the spoon ready." She found the stirring spoon that she had put aside, and plunged it into some of the white pudding. When it held a giant's mouthful, she stained the white with the red granular gravy of the beans and added a few beans on top. Gingerly, she lifted the decorated spoon and presented it to the girl's mother.

Katayi had been behind the scenes all day. At this moment she was at the forefront, regretfully holding the spoon, still obliged to wait for the midwife. The midwife grabbed the largest platter—both cassava and beans—lifted it, and started forward. Katayi followed her, and in a flash all the women picked up their dishes and fell in behind. The procession rushed to the milk tree, and a great whistling and hooting went up as the onlookers jumped and peered. Lifting her dish high in the air the midwife ran around the milk tree. The procession followed her, then the mother held up the spoon. They all roared in chorus:

> Here she comes,
> The Many-Budding Tree,
> Hers is the child,
> Hers is the child!

This was Katayi's single instant; she shouted, "Who wants cassava from the Many-Budding Tree?" and flourished the spoon for the last time. Evita the hooker rushed forward, arrived first amid a jostle of competitors, seized the spoon, and bounced with triumph.

Manyosa was at my elbow. "The one who grabs the spoon is the hyena who comes to snatch the girl-child. Those beans are the hyena spots. We just hope it's a local 'hyena,' or we may never see our child again. Young men are always snatching off our girls to marry them. The ones who live in an unknown village often turn out to be sorcerers, if not monsters. So you see why we don't like it. Of course, the winner gets to eat the spoonful; it will give her many children. You'll always be ready to come if you eat beans." She gave me a long-faced smile. "That's why they rush for the spoon."

The crowd sat on the grass in groups, each with a plate in the center. Manyosa bustled about, organizing the concourse according to villages of origin. Sani, Mangaleshi's daughter, with a new dress pulled down over her straight chest, plumped herself down by the dish allocated to Kajima.

"Hold back, you bad-mannered thing!" Manyosa reproved her. "First the elders."

Manyosa drew me toward the dish. It was a feast for women. "Come on, Mishy, have a bit. Let's see you eat cassava."

I scooped a piece off the main pudding. It felt warm and soft in my hand. The others, I noticed, were setting to. They plunged in, with smooth clean hands that never touched food until they had been washed. With much agility the fingers withdrew a piece, shaped it into a knob, passed it into the bean juice; then, quickly and decently, the knob was popped whole into the willing mouth and swallowed with one mouthing around, while the hand already was bringing up another knob, already bean-juiced. The mouth was never shut between mouthfuls, an honest mouth, open as the day. I looked about before trying my piece, then looked down again guiltily. English etiquette told me I shouldn't watch people eating.

It was somewhat like eating wallpaper paste or the edge of a wet slice of bread. I liked the warmth. I started to chew, a mistake. The odor of a rotting pool burst forth, the pool where the cassava was soaked. Hooding my eyes, I swallowed, then looked around. People were still eating. I started another piece, rolling it a little in my white hand, against which the cassava looked gray. This time I swallowed at once, and had a warm, filled feeling inside. Manyosa was looking at me.

"I've had enough," I told her. "Thank you."

"Good, good," she approved. "You will learn to eat." I couldn't look at her.

At the milk tree, three women still wearily stomped around, preserving the honor of the sacred place. A host of dishes had been set out to feed groups that spread right along the margin of the plain. I could see each group flanked by trusting yet watchful children, who were awaiting their turn. A quiet rustling pervaded the field. Dust lay everywhere; the grass was trampled and soiled. I noticed abandoned bits of rag that had been used to wipe babies. A little further off I could see the backs of two young dandies in smart clothes, tennis shoes, and shiny red belts, who were wolfishly eyeing a couple of elegant wives from town in purple and green kirtles. The girls stretched their necks and laughed at the boys, then turned away, overcome.

"Get up now," said Manyosa, helping me to my feet. "The dance is going to end very soon, and then we'll do the carrying."

We stood together on the field. The sun was striking tired and level through the forest, its light churned into a long swithering haze around the milk tree. Everyone was streaming back to the central spot. Mwenda lay there still. She had not replied to her friends' teasing, had not stretched or changed position; she lay slack and absent from the daytime world. I started forward, and found myself beside the forgotten bush, the forgotten bundle, now surrounded by the midwife and her helpers. The women looked perturbed, as if they faced the job of digging out a seed lying on the ground. It might have taken root there, it was already fecund. When the Ndembu place millet gruel in a certain calabash, it will seed all over with the beer ferment. Mwenda was like that now.

Manyosa said: "The place where Guinea Fowl lies is the Place of Death, Ifwilu. There she has lost everything, there she has suffered. She believes that she is dead. She cannot walk to her seclusion hut, she must be carried. Do you know what would happen if she fell to earth? All her desire would be lost, she would be dead to her husband's love." I looked at Manyosa gravely.

The midwife by the antelope skin looked away down through the forest. The sun was fading—faded while we watched—beneath the forest mazes. God would not be embarrassed by what we did, now that evening was here.

Now the tempo changes. I can hear the midwife ordering the small boys to be off; boys, the elders with the drums, the sun, god, all must be absent, only women now. The midwife is already raising Mwenda by the armpits, along with the blanket still drooping over her head. The other women hedge us in thickly. For a moment Mwenda stands like a statue, her form vague under the blanket. The midwife places her hand on Mwenda's head: "Not born yet, still dead, little one!" Then at once she turns and heaves Mwenda onto her back. I can see Mwenda's arms for a moment, passively clasped about the good woman's throat. The other women notice and hastily cover them over. Arms must not be born first.

Meanwhile, the midwife beckons impatiently with her foot, nudging the antelope skin.

"The Bedding Grass, give it here," she tells them. They lift the skin and gather a wad of grass from where Mwenda has been lying, the grass that mice gather to lap around their nests to shelter their young. At the end of the journey, Mwenda, too, will be sheltered. The grass is thrust into Mwenda's hand under the blanket. I can see the outline of her fist, clutching hard.

The women swirl around, some spreading out and bringing in boughs from the bush, which they place around the milk tree to protect it from damage. The arrow, the arrow! They take up the arrow and the beads. Then all the women meet at the milk tree with an upsurge of excitement, and hands flash in, each picking a leaf, each one a deep green milk-exuding leaf.

Manyosa pushes me forward: "A leaf, Mishy, quick, we are going!" Now I hold one of my own. I touch the white globule at the end of the stalk. Sticky. They all start singing a jaunty song. Manyosa nudges me urgently: "Close your hand, Mishy, hide it. Oops! You must never let it be seen like that." I shut my hand promptly; the song chants the command, "Close up! Keep in! Magic!" The crowd closes right around the midwife, proudly carrying her covered burden. Everyone is grinning uncontrollably. The body of women moves, thickly surrounding the burden, each of us with a shoulder tense, the leaf hidden in a fist. Singing breaks out as we sway toward the village. Now we reach the opening-out of the bush.

Men have started to run hither and thither, gathering drums into a group. Kajima stands in the midst of them, his white head erect. His face is at peace, a sign of great emotion. As we are about to cross into the circular ground, the midwife hesitates. She is marking time; I realize she has been dancing with the weight of the girl on her back. She smiles at everyone and all the women pack themselves backwards around the girl, an angry swarm of bees guarding the queen. A hum, a hiss seems to go through the pack. Up she hoists the girl still higher, the brown blanket heaves above the crowd, and we plunge on, jigging one, two, three, four, with Manyosa showing me the step. Faces flash outward as we press toward the drums, toward the men. Again we come to a halt, bodies tripping and lifting to gather into a smaller area, becoming one thick body, a great wild animal that advances upon the village, right up to the men. Slowly, slowly we make the round of the drums, one shoulder leading in toward the girl. The men, their heads held high, shout the song back at us and crack at us with their drums. Vic is there with them and my heart leaps. They are admiring us!

In the midst of these birth pangs, the girl has nearly arrived. One stretch of ground remains ahead, and the seclusion hut comes into sight. Our speed increases. We turn toward the hut, letting the midwife with her burden pass into the front. The last steps are a march. A swing, and the midwife is already staggering her burden down at the entrance of the hut. She turns right around backwards and sinks to the ground among the crowd. Mwenda has vanished within like a bubble off the end of an arm; gone, a complete negative, but safe. A great hoot goes up from the crowd.

Manyosa turns to me in triumph. "It's done!" she shouts above the din; our thrilled eyes meet.

Suddenly I'm being tugged, pulled forward. We leave the hut in a rush.

"Race, race!" cries Manyosa. "The leaves! To the mother's hut!"

We sprint in a frantic mass across the plaza, clutching the milk leaves in our closed palms.

"And first around the men," pants Manyosa. We're all strung out, racing around the men. Then to the mother's hut, the thatch! Evita the hooker gets there first, raising her arm where we all must reach, into the thatch. In go the leaves, tucked in cozily, each leaf a baby for Mwenda. I spin away, out of breath and suddenly puzzled. Mwenda was the baby, wasn't she, born backward into her hut?

I frowned. When they plucked the leaves, what was actually happening? The leaves were taken from the "family tree" that would give life to Mwenda in the future, a kind of immortality. She and the tree were identified; the leaves were the children of the tree. Like Mwenda, the leaves were carried into the village under cover, in the care of all the women; the leaves were put in a straw roof, but this was the mother's roof. The women delivered the future children to the mother; but the future bride, intervening between mother and grandchildren, had been taken away, born inward into invisibility, not outward to the world. The women took her away for themselves, she was their baby, not her mother's, a baby in sex, borne in the stages of sex by her nurses, in absence from the village.

I knew there was more to it even than that. Under the dark trees the dark green leaves were displayed. They glowed over her through the whole day of dancing, while she was "dead," nothing. The leaves were her children, as yet unplucked, unfuturized, "moving about in worlds not realized," as in Wordsworth's poem. We performed in the world of the imagination. For Guinea Fowl was a vacuum, drawing the future. The physical seed within her, with its half of a flower, was cold and dark, she was still nothing. The women were needed now. Mwenda at this stage could not belong to any particular person, she belonged to the whole of life. The women in a great social body had to take over: imagination had outrun us all, had outrun the present, so that no single woman was strong enough to make the journey into the future alone. But in that body we could do it. Magic, the powerful tool of the imagination, was needed; we could perform the future. Together we encompassed this mystery, the future, the plunge into empty space that is marriage, and then children; we could bear the child, and even the children of the child, while nothing yet had been proved. There was no marriage, no children.

These were the elements: the sacred tree, the darkened girl, the huge group animal that took the future generation on board and traveled over like an ark to the other side. The ark was the vehicle of Mwenda's power. The midwife was the commander, the entrepreneur of the whole undertaking. The composite vehicle, all of it bearing leaves, and the Guinea Fowl borne, being quickened with futurity that was not real, all believed together. At the hut the bubble seemed to vanish, yet we had won a life.

And there was that superb gesture to the shy miserable mother, who had herself suffered with the daughter all day, robbed as a mother, and banned; why, she might have wanted to take her daughter through adolescence herself. Yet had she done so, social warmth would have begun to fade and Mwenda's life would have run backwards. Even so, it was to the mother that the mass of women turned in its hour of triumph. We held the bonds, ours was the power of continuance, but it was for Katayi's benefit: to the mother we granted the future, we bequeathed her those great new allies, grandchildren.

Manyosa expressed this continuance when she dressed Mpeza, her baby granddaughter, in beads and paraded her around the village on the occasion of her first tooth. Nyachitela did it by a curious jumping of the generations; she couldn't remember the difference between her daughter's initiation and her own. And why did this milk tree rite mean so much to me, as well as to Manyosa and Nyachitela? It was because the girl in me persisted. Something like the milk tree is continuously fertile in me, something at that long-ago point of change that said "young leaves," "excitement," "opening up," and "milk." And I, as old as I may grow, will always be the young girl that I was, and feel the hopeful female soul inside permanently growing in my body, just as an old tree comes out with its absurd young buds year after year.

There really was a girl in the A-frame hut, because I used to visit her. The women were teaching her to dance; she could make her breasts shiver—those naked teats, all swollen up like the fat buds of a tropical tree, very tender and fragile. The women were proud of her, the tall subservient beauty with the peaceful face.

The women now worked on her body, carefully patterning it with cicatrizations, tiny raised stipples on her breasts and belly and labia. These became areas for the bridegroom's fingers to play, as a blind man feels braille. Seen naked, her body was a work of art. Even more carefully they gave her sexual training, until enjoyment was of a high order.

The three months soon passed; Guinea Fowl's training was finished, and she was ready to perform and become a woman. I joined my friends in the early morning as they approached Guinea Fowl's hut, trilling high. Guinea Fowl knew what day it was, so she demonstrated what she had been taught, writhing and circulating her hips in the full refinement of her skill. Then the women went in singing, and Natalie took her up on her back, again covered with her blanket, and we danced out, this time to a screened area behind Natalie's hut called the Shaving Place. They set her down, took off her blanket, and began to work on her; she sat meek and quiet all the while.

A strong camaraderie developed behind the screen as we sensed the beauty we were creating. This was my idea of it:

> Origin blue, the sky. A new task comes today—to make a woman out of dust, and dirty blanket, and fear.
>
> Take the child out of her hiding place, keep her low, limp-limbed, in the corner of a screen, while the women make Woman.
>
> Her head is ours, the matted hair emerges; with a handmade comb we carve out its quarters, and turn that shag into a rhythmic idol.

> Ours is her body. Utterly her naked self opens to warm water.
> Hand over hand, every grown woman takes off her
> beadstring and gives it her.

> Within, her liver whitens with pride, but still she obeys, grave
> of face.

The morning advanced. As they prepared Mwenda the women sang initiation songs and a heroicomic ballad about the black schoolmaster who robbed the missionary, an old church elder known as Long Pole, who kept the Sunday collection in his desk because "he no undastanda tha bank!" When they had washed and shaved Mwenda the women brought forward the tub-chested little attendant, the "firekindler," who was with Mwenda in seclusion. She, too, was cleansed.

A small calabash bowl was brought that contained a rolling pink oil, natural castor oil. They scooped it out with fluid gestures and slithered it all over the naked Mwenda, down into the cicatrized places of her body. Finally they upturned the bowl over her head, flooding the delicate braiding with oil. Now she sat with her fists meekly turned inward, closed in, held to her temples. The next cosmetic was a platter heaped with dark ruddy earth known as ngula, the clotted blood of circumcision. On occasions different from this one, it was called mukundu, the witches' war paint. This was Mwenda's body paint. The women rubbed it in with the oil, sculpting her, highlighting her, matting her with deep red glowing earthiness. They pressed it into the beautiful braids, molding and raising the hair into a heavy earthen crown.

Within the part glimmered a tiny string of white beads; I had seen them hiding it there. They had lifted it quickly and surreptitiously out of a little white bowl of water, where it was attached to a tiny twig. "Shall I tell her?" Manyosa asked Natalie.

"Go ahead, old friend. Mishy's one of us now."

Manyosa bent toward me. "This twig is a bow, a tiny bow like the hunter's bow. The string of beads is called kasenzi. It's the spirit of the lineage of mothers, the spirit of the girl's own fertility, which is coming alive at this time to bless the village. Now look! The bow holds the arrow, the arrow is contained in it, and by the power of that bow, it shoots!"

I remembered the arrow, the long dangerous weapon belonging to the bridegroom that had been set upright in the ground when the girl had first been placed under the milk tree. The arrow had been hung with that same tiny row of white beads draped over the notch and the feathers. Mwenda had not seen them; she had been "dead" when they had rested there, a tiny string of beads at the point where the arrow strains against the power of the string. During the seclusion dance this arrow had been thrust, not into some bloodied animal, but in the milk tree ground, at the root of the lineage. When Mwenda was finally lifted away from the milk tree, charged in her state of fertile death, Natalie snatched the white beads and carried them, as Mwenda was carried, to the hut shaped like a crotch. There they had been quickly concealed in the apex. From that time on, all through her training, the girl was forbidden to look up at the apex where the two beams of milk wood and blood wood met. Like the milk tree, the blood tree was an important living form. When it was slashed, its gum, red as mahogany, flowed in coagulating gouts. The Ndembu used it as a rafter for the girl's shelter, just as her blood would later be used for her child.

On the occasion of the cleansing ritual, the white beads were privately extracted, washed, and quickly hidden, as I watched, in the part beneath the masses of earth on Mwenda's head. If those beads were seen by strange men with their evils and powers, the women would wail as if a death had occurred or the miscarriage of an unborn child. On the night of consummation, the girl would undo the earthen crown and show her husband these beads, already spiritually fertilized by his arrow in the ground of initiation.

After the white beads had been concealed in Mwenda's hair, the women placed around her head a band of colored beads like a tiara. Then they arranged more beads over the top, further covering the sacred white ones. Necklaces were passed over her shoulders and under each arm so that they crossed in front, above and below her naked breasts. Her little sister, who had been her firekindler, was brought forward, and she, too, was decorated with beads. Then the child was placed in a circle of women who watched to see if she could perform the heel drumming dance. Her tiny body sailed around with only the hips and hands and feet in motion, her face as serene and grave as an elder's.

Mwenda was now fully prepared. She stood naked above the waist, wrapped below with an ample cloth drawn up between her legs and strung around her waist so that it hung over in a wide dancing skirt. The wrapping between her legs protected the place of her fiery longing. The white beads were well hidden, for Mwenda, being delicate and beautiful, was particularly open to sorcery this day. She sat down and they brought her white chicken meat and white cassava pudding. Her fists were still humbly closed, and she took the food like a baby, straight into her mouth from the women's hands. After she had finished, the others could eat, beginning with the tiny children and my little Rene, the daughters of us all.

At last the midwife rises. "Hooloo-hooloo-hooloo-hooloo!" she calls to the village. The drums from the shelter reply in a joyous crash, and the whole group of women breaks out around the screen and advances upon the village. The midwife bursts out before them, waving an ax and hooting. Behind, there is a jostle. Guinea Fowl has disappeared, led away. I look around, still excited, but puzzled. We advance and form a circle before the drums; all the men are grinning with great excitement. Some people have been approaching the circle from far over the other side, coming from the bush; we cannot see who it is, there is a mat held in the way.

Now through the dust of the crowd we can see. It is Guinea Fowl! She penetrates into the circle like an animal, head first, stooping—a baby, a newborn spirit, from an unexpected direction. She pads across the ring, right up to the crowd, and butts her head against the women there. They turn around to the side and enlarge the circle to surround her. She is bent quite low, and bangs the ground with legs harnessed in rattles. She gropes grotesquely toward the drums, spits into her hand, and touches the drum. The drums thunder. She springs right up, right upright. Ah, her breasts are ripe. Her hand is raised, gracefully fanning a black swirl of animal hair over her shoulder; it is Headman Kajima's own eland tail switch, his lordly badge of office. She is one rapid vibration from heel to skirt to breast, breasts flashing up and down, head falling languorously from side to side. Even her back is jingling, for now she is wearing a back pad stitched all over with bells, which she contrives to flick up and down like her breasts; the bells ring and jingle and clatter in the enormous vibration focused at that spot. She seems to be an orchestra in full swing, she and the drums and the frenzied singing. All the while her face is serene, with just a touch of ecstasy.

The crowd watches, singing its praises, clapping in time. A jostle continually thrusts everyone forward, as someone adds a penny to a dish for the midwife who has organized such a marvel. Guinea Fowl takes a cloth, dances with it, and hands it to the headman, her fertility for the village. She veers away and seizes a gun. The crowd hoots. She points the gun and dances with it on her shoulder; she is the hunter who brings meat to the village. Then she dances in fancy up a tree, and descends running with honey from the beehive, licking the honey off her arm. She pulls her hand sharply away—a sting—but dances on: Guinea Fowl has no fear. She dances as if wading through water, bending over a cloth full of imaginary fish. Emerging from the stream, she hands the bounty around the village. Women hoot and rush forward to place pennies atop her head. Yet her face remains impassive. The midwife retrieves the pennies and hoots of praise resound. At last Guinea Fowl stands, strong, sweating, quiet, with slender brown shoulders like a boy's that sway to and fro. The midwife takes the tall girl by the hand and leads her away to the bridegroom's hut.

Late in the evening Vic and I walked down the road by Kajima. The mulundu bird whistled softly among the shadows; he was calling "I love you so-o." The village was quiet and cool, and we returned to it in a dream. Vic's shoulders touched mine as we walked side by side to our hut. It was sweet that we had learned to get married, somehow.

The mind's eye follows Mwenda into her husband's hut, much as Manyosa related the events of her own marriage.

There she goes, nodding with her heavy mudded head. Still full of pride and heat, she is carried to the door of the hut, where her husband is sitting. She must not look at the doorway, for it is the doorway to her womb; so she is thrust in backwards and set down on the bed. As she sinks down, her husband stands up, erect. Now Natalie pushes something into the ground by the bed. It quivers there upright on its blade: it is the milk tree arrow, his arrow, which the midwife tended throughout Mwenda's seclusion.

"Now if this wonder-man would be so good as to pay me a shilling, I have something of interest for him outside this door."

"Sixpence, you old witch."

"Hm." Then, to Mwenda, "Well, I'll be off, my dear, with my calabash of beer."

"Orh!" he pleads. "Please, my dear madam, do not take it away. Here is your shilling." She brings in a fragrant calabash of kachai.

"My children," she says, sighing; it is the end of her efforts. "I have done all I can for you: now it is up to you."

Darkness journeys over the forest. Late in the night the midwife has a last secret ritual to perform; she tiptoes from door to door around the village. "Coolness, coolness," she murmurs, laying something before each door. And then she is gone. The fragment left behind lies running with its own wetness, a little black sponge, nothing but a scrap of river mud, a small symbol of rain and seriousness. Marriages are made of the deep running of the river, the cool gray rain, serious as a baby's devoted sucking.

Night reigns over the village. Within the hut Mwenda is mild. Reaching down, Makanjila, her good man, unties the waist string from her hips, and the skirt slips down. Now she is dancing on the bed, circulating, making delicious his first advance, forgetting that she had ever doubted her body in the days before initiation. He enters, caressing around as he enters; she faints, she faints, she is totally gone, as if turned into someone else, one with him. Afterwards, she lies on her back for a long time and hardly needs to breathe in her contentment.

It is morning. Mwenda lays her hands upon her head and fingers the long groove between the braids to clear it of the red earth. Makanjila looks down, and gradually he sees the white beads that no other man shall see. She gives them to him, her palms open at last.

"Coming now!" rasps the voice of the midwife outside, the first voice of the new era. The old woman rattles the straw door and fusses in.

"Dearie, let's just see." She goes to Mwenda and feels at her side. "Hm, Hm. That's all right then." She nods joyfully. Mwenda has put in her hand a wet piece of cloth, sticky with semen.

The old woman brings them a chicken, boiled in a black pot. They eat it, juice and all, smiling at each other while they gently suck the bones. Each bone they replace carefully in the pot. Mwenda looks around to make sure none is left out.

"Careful, there's one," she says. "Oops, don't break it!"

The bridegroom picks it up and puts it in. The midwife collects the pot of bones and rushes it to the hopeful mother in her hut. These unbroken relics stand for the future children, complete and beautiful. The marriage has begun.

THE BOTTOM OF THE YEAR

ONE THURSDAY WE WENT, as we often did on our days off, to picnic down by the stream, leaving the car, which was now defunct, under a rotting garage roof. We jammed food into a basket and walked out of the camp, making our way through Kajima with eyes half shut in case we encountered an important visitor on his way to greet us with the ever-compelling calabash of beer. It had been a hard week. We kept on over the road and into the bush on the other side, where we felt safer. Freddy went in front with the basket clamped down on his head in the way he had learnt from his friends. After him ran Rene in a tattered dress, chattering in a gay little voice, to which we responded tiredly if at all. Then came Bobby, trotting back and forth like a puppy. Vic and I walked side by side behind them, straddling a path that had been made by people walking in single file. While going along we kept up a running battle about who should walk in front. Vic said I should, but I refused. He was about to make a rejoinder when Rene came to an unexpected halt.

"Ouch! Ouch!" she cried. We stumbled over her and swore. Rene stood stock still, huddled into herself.

"Something's wrong with the kid. Oh. Ants." We disgustedly gave right of way to the ants now obvious in large numbers at our feet. Vic grabbed Rene and yanked her off the path to a safer spot, where we got to work on the ants clinging to her and, by this time, to us. They were red army ants.

"Rene," I accused her. "Why ever do you just stand there? Look at them all."

The sinister line moved along the ground, slender as an unrolled ball of rust-colored knitting yarn, but shaggier. Vic bent down to look; he loved ants. The creatures were straddling their leggy bodies over their road, making a matted arch, a patchy tube to protect their comrades inside bearing eggs. The road traveled along, wavered, passed under logs, shivered across open ground, disappeared, and reappeared in a wide detour around a nest of tiny fierce black ants before it returned, exactly to where we stood.

"There're some coming for you, Vic." Vic clapped his hand to his privates. He reached into his pants, quickly found the hard stubborn little insect, and threw it down. Once again we had to remove to another place; then we spotted where the ant's road had been broken in the first place. The roadmakers were swirling around in an angry circle. Vic carefully lifted Rene over the spot to have a look. "If you walk on their road they get savage. And if they bite, run! Don't just stand there." How could we know the real trouble? Rene needed glasses and couldn't focus on anything as small as an ant.

I was frightened. "Oh, Vic, supposing we hadn't been there. She'd have been a clean-picked skeleton." He took my arm and I crept my hand into his.

We left the stinging matted thread to itself and made our way to the right, off the path and toward a wooded valley through which ran the Nyalufanta, a tributary of the Kakula. We broke into the open further down and jumped the brook, which was no wider than a man's body. The other side was known as hunters' bush. As we set foot on the far bank, the trees before us suddenly were spanned by a light brown arch, then another. A thud reached us. Two large animals in the woods were leaping with fright. We glimpsed sloping rumps and flap tails bounding in a precipitate escape. Afterwards, I remembered the long strength of their backs as they arched.

"Duiker antelope, right?" I said to Vic.

"Yes. But they're early if they hope to find any wild plum leaves." The trees were quite bare.

We wandered up the bank and, entering the forest, found a dry gully, where we sat down on the fallen leaves facing home. It was a little warmer now. The forest stood behind us, huge, black, burnt in patches, mournfully uninhabited, stretching away and away into Angola. We sat with our hands still on our food basket. The silence was complete. A tiny bend of the Kakula could be seen far down between the trees; no women were hoeing there yet. When we had set out the morning had been cold, for it was still early in the year and the spring had not yet arrived. The sky was hazy with the constant forest burning that was carried on to encourage the young grass and to attract antelope. The stream was running on its old capital, gradually draining the land; it had not rained for many months. At the bottom of the year, sitting in our dry gully, we rested; and as the sun slowly veered around the sky we saw that spring was there if one would see it. The twigs of the trees were tender, the breath from the valley was warm and stinging. The sky stood over the flat treetops, yellowly blue. We took pencils and wrote poetry. Then we rested, almost miserable at the loneliness and freedom, the not-knowing-whither of everything.

A month later I wandered down another of the bush trails to find where the Ndembu grew their cash crops, following my path across the motor road and into the forest on the other side. After a while the forest sloped downhill, becoming quite steep, until the path gave a turn and opened out onto a slope facing a wide space. I stopped. Before me lay a valley, blue with sky and distance, with a glint of the Kakula River in its midst. The trees beside me contrived to frame the scene with the vermilion leaves of spring, soft sprays in every color of red. I touched a trunk: it was sooty from some previous bushburning. From where I stood to the distant forest wall at the other side of the valley was about a mile, a mile of sunshine. The land was curdled into great areas of black and great areas of green, black where the greedy hoes of the women were honeycombing the ground into seed mounds, green where the young swamp was still growing wild. One, two, three, four women could be seen dotted across the plain, each on her own patch.

I made my way down the plunging path between reeds and over mud stretches, deep into the heady smell of wet rushes. I passed some recently hoed mounds, each with its sprout of corn consisting of just a few wide leaves at this stage. The mounds belonged to a scraggy beldame with greedy eyes called Nyawunyumbi, which I had better translate for the reader as She-Jackal. She-Jackal was standing by her boundary arguing with Nyachitela the Kajima witch, whose garden was next to hers. She-Jackal's squeaking voice alternated with Nyachitela's baleful complaints. The dispute concerned the ownership of the mound between them. In the end they lifted up their hoes and slashed the mound in two, each creating a small extra mound on her own side. I made my greetings and walked slowly around the gardens, counting my steps. I drew She-Jackal's plot on my sketch pad, with the idea of mapping the whole valley. Moving to the next plot, I shouted to She-Jackal to find out who the owner was. She-Jackal came over, full of information. Her naming of this plot and that eventually led the two of us right to the far side of the valley where the path wandered under the shade of an enormous barrier of glowing evergreen trees. From inside the thicket we could hear the sound of the river, lapping, lapping. We passed on to make our way through mounds left over from last year. Here our legs sank in deep, for the dips between the mounds had been burnt over and were half in water covered with scum. One of my ancient walking shoes stayed behind when I lifted out my foot with a squelch.

"Bother," I said, and dragged the shoe out. We escaped to the top of the mound, looking at our legs. Mine wore long socks of black, while She-Jackal's slender root-like ankles and legs, slithered with the same mud, looked gray against her black skin.

"It's too wet here, Mishy," she twittered, and I agreed. We turned aside to wash our legs in the river where it issued from the trees. The stream was coursing neatly along in its sinuous half-cylinder of channel, white below and clear all through down to the bottom. We stood for a while in the water watching the fish panic away; a great crab sank even further under a stone. We waded across, almost fearful in the middle where the current bore along. Staggering to the side, we sat watching the water as it raged like emotion around and away, elbowing an incomprehensible course all over the fertile valley.

She-Jackal stayed with me all that day. I paced and counted and sketched and wrote, and She-Jackal led me on. At last, when my paper was smudged with graphite and peat, I stopped. She-Jackal came over to look at the map. "Wonderful," she squeaked, puzzled at those small shapes on the paper. What had they to do with the river valley?

We walked home, warm in the cheekbones from the late evening sun, cool in the fingers from the last rinse in the river. At the camp I gave She-Jackal two shillings, which made her really happy. I was happy, too, for I had found someone with a sufficiently powerful urge for work and money to stick to a job.

Another day She-Jackal and I visited the old village site of Kajima near the Nyalufanta, Kakula's tributary; the site now was used for peanuts, which were doing well on the old kitchen middens. I walked over to one of the masses of green and bent down to look, never having seen peanut plants before. I lifted up the stalks and found that their growing tips were embedded in the dirt. I tugged, and peanut shells emerged from the

ground, fat and heavy, clinging to the tips. When I looked up
again, I was staggered by the view of the radiant river jungle.

"Lupinda lived here," said She-Jackal. She stood upright, gazing out at the stretches of grass. I spoke quietly, for it seemed
that the ancient houses were still there, and that old Nyishi
Chandenda, the long dead headman, and his brother Lupinda,
hunter of renown, might rise from some shadowy chota and
require our greetings. Gray soil, bracken, double-fronded
ground fruit stems grew far and near; but no hut, not a spar
remained.

THE FISH EAGLE

IT WAS SEPTEMBER, and one of the two midsummers that occur in the tropics was nearly upon us. The heat was a torture, and now Manyosa fell ill. Not only did her eyes bulge more than ever, but a goiter on her neck was dragging her down. This was hyperthyroidism, caused by lack of iodine in the diet. Manyosa drooped about the village, sometimes coming to my hut with mournful staring eyes to share a pot of tea. I spoke seriously to her about an operation, but Manyosa would make no move. At last the village began to feel her misery. Even those who had tried to help her felt guilty, and mutual accusations brewed up in the chota until finally a Tukuka ritual, literally "Shaking," was arranged for her. Evita the hooker was to be principal woman doctor, with Nsimba her pimp husband as master of ceremonies.

I learned that the Shaking ritual was a modern up-to-date possession rite. Vic and I were both aware of the wide distribution of shaking and trembling phenomena in spirit possession rites, but we had never been close to one before. Musona and certain other informants used to denigrate the Shaking ritual—it was newfangled, from Angola, not an Ndembu ritual at all, and so on. I could have argued that falling in the spirit occurred in their own Ihamba ritual, in Kayongu, the initiation of doctors, and others. There always seems to exist an antipossession, anti-mysticism faction in every religious community, as in Christianity, Judaism, Islam, or Buddhism.

Nsimba was hardly the respectable parson. He was a charming fellow in a long black coat that flapped and swung against his bare legs; the coat boasted an astrakhan collar, which accentuated Nsimba's high forehead and the folds of self-admiration around his mouth, folds telling of his preoccupation with women and their desirable bodies. Somehow they constituted the sex smile; his name, Nsimba, meant genet cat, "sex cat." Genet cats defecate in the same place each day and their scent glands give off a smell of semen.

An enormous fire was built outside Manyosa's hut. They brought up the drums and Nsimba led the raucous singing. As I sat in the circle I heard muttering among the women: a European spirit was making Manyosa ill. I was anxious, and leaned over toward Master Kajima. "Would that be one of our family?" I asked.

"No, Mishy. You have children of your own. You're no witch, you've too much to lose yourself."

The voices continued worrying at the question.

"A spirit from the Congo? From Angola?" Even an African from those advanced territories was regarded as a European. Nsimba himself came from Bié, an Angolan province. "Ah, those wonderful drinks we had in Bié," he used to say, shaking his head. I pictured a colorful cantina, with Nsimba in its midst belting out lewd songs in his deep bass. My eyes refocused on the scene before me: the fire, the medicine pots, the occasional burst of drums, Manyosa stripped to the waist, so central there and unembarrassed.

The murmuring went on.

Nyamuvwila, the first wife of Kajima, had an opinion. She was an oldish woman with projecting teeth, said to be sly, a true Malabu. Her eyebrows went up in the middle, giving her a deprecating expression.

"Nsimba," she called, leaning over. "I know the witch. It's that daughter-in-law of Manyosa. She has an Angolan spirit. Isn't she an Ovimbundu girl from Angola? Why did Manyosa's boy make such a bad marriage? She's just a tramp."

The crowd chewed over that one.

Chikasa, Manyosa's husband, a short man, climbed onto a log to make a peroration. "It's the spirit of Manyosa's father," he announced in a squeaky voice. "No one talks about him, ever. He gives me the shivers. Didn't he die all alone?" Chikasa got down from his perch and whispered for a moment to Chautongi. Chikasa's face was long with important information, his eyebrows were raised, and his eyes shifted like a politician's.

"He was tried for murdering his wife's lover. Maybe his ghost has a resentment against his wife's daughter."

Chautongi's eyes glinted horribly, as if she had swallowed a snake. She was known as a gossip and as a Christian convert.

The process of investigation went on. Manyosa sat waiting in the center with her legs straight out before her. I could see her old breasts drooping as far as her waist. Now she herself began to speak.

"People of mine, kinsfolk," she said, raising mournful eyes. "I am afflicted with dreams. I see a child all painted red who flies down from the air. When he touches me I die. It is worse than the sickness of my heavy neck, and I cannot escape it."

Many feet shifted and eyes glanced to and fro.

"Mishy here says I should go to the European hospital on the copperbelt, so that the doctor can cut . . . cut . . ." She couldn't speak, but made a gesture across her throat. "That doctor is very wonderful. But he lives far away, over a hundred hills and a hundred streams. I will die on the journey. No. I have been called by the Shaking spirit and must receive him before I go." Her face looked delicate and pathetic, like that of a small girl.

On hearing her words the crowd rallied and the drummers returned to their drums. A rank of women doctors, able and dominating, armed with their rattles, sat against the fire, while darkness gathered around them. Manyosa waited, her face troubled and excited. To launch the proceedings they chalked white crosses all over her body. She sat open to them all with her hands open, palms upward, and face full of uncertainty. The drums stuttered their appeals aloft and song broke out. Manyosa was shivering slightly in the cooling breeze; was she cold? Then I noticed Evita the hooker at the other side of the circle, shaking violently and rhythmically, with an intentional yet compulsive movement of her body. She was in trance. This wasn't the vain Evita now; she was practicing her real gift, and it had taken over. Was this what happened at the old-time Quaker meetings, I wondered, when the Friends were visited by the Holy Spirit? Perhaps it was.

Just beyond, another woman was caught by the same power. Her arms were up and she was dancing the airplane, vibrating her hands in a marvelous imitation of a propellor. Everyone stood up and trilled. After a while Kandaleya, who was one of the doctors, shook her rattle by the ear of the possessed woman to relieve her of the spirit, a compassionate gesture.

The doctors turned back to Manyosa. "Shake, shake, Manyosa," they cried; Manyosa was barely swaying, cold.

"Rattling-thud, rattling-thud, drubbedy drubbedy drubbedy drubbedy—yey, yey-yey yey!" went the frantic sound. Shaking and rattling they conveyed a pot of medicine to Manyosa's lips; she drank. Kandaleya benevolently leaned toward her and spat in blessing on her brow; Nsimba took a bunch of leaves and used it to spray her with medicine from a large pot. Manyosa sat melancholy and swaying. How they hooted to raise a quiver in her! The spirit was not coming, the spirit was not coming. Evita frowned; she had come out of her trance. Kajima conferred with Nsimba, who nodded, a sentertious expression on his face.

Chautongi was suddenly inspired. "Manyosa has received the Holy Spirit. She has been caught by Jesus Christ from above." The crowd turned to her, puzzled but impressed. Could that be the trouble?

Then all started speaking at once, declaring that no, they had divined the wrong spirit in the first place. It was a hunter's spirit they must drum for. They changed songs without hesitation and started calling out of the patient the mystic tooth of the hunter's ghost. Manyosa sat humble and swaying. All at once everyone turned in my direction: right from under where I was standing, Nyamuvwila's head appeared, rolling up from where it had suddenly flopped sideways, and in an instant the head had gone over to the other side in an immense swing of the body. I shook with astonishment. Nyamuvwila's undulations continued, flop, flop, flop, from one side to the other, faster and faster, as the hunter's drum rhythm swelled out and the hunter's spirit thrilled through her. The new theme was striking a chord in her, a response from an unexpected quarter. A small smile of pride crept around her lips even in the midst of her convulsions, for Nyamuvwila, the innocent-browed, sly servile wife of the headman, was now able to show exactly how she felt. Her affliction? It was leprosy.

Now the fun started. Eyes lit up, heads were turned this way and that to catch the next manifestation of the spirit. Hoots of encouragement broke out, for Manyosa herself was roundly swaying. Nsimba regarded her for a moment, then put a large bowl of water before her. Manyosa swayed again, again, again; she rose up on her knees; she bent forward; the drums swept flights of bullets out here, out there; she swayed nearer and yet nearer to the water in front of her, first one side, then the other side, then—splash—she was in it, sweeping gouts of water violently out with her head, back, forth, back, forth, her body helplessly following the controlling sweep of possession. Nsimba followed the gyrations with a supporting hand.

I looked at my old friend sorrowfully. This faculty of hers turned her into a stranger. Where was she? In a religious ecstasy whose colors I could not see, colors that left the world more gray because they had all the glory. My will went out in my eyes to drag Manyosa back; what I wanted was some acknowledgement, a knowing smile or a sign of some sort. But Manyosa was impervious, safe in her glory.

Everyone was on her feet. "What does it mean?" I turned to ask, but I had no teacher. Manyosa was my teacher. I took a desperate breath, spun around, and found Mangaleshi by my side. "Mangaleshi . . ."

"Do you see it? Do you see it?" she demanded. "The bird spirit? Manyosa's fish eagle? See how it swoops and dives under the water!" Yes, I could see it now.

Then the doctors took over. Evita held out her rattle and placed it firmly over Manyosa's breast, butt down, then pressed the rampant head with it. Like static electricity the power ran off and Manyosa grew still.

A fish eagle, bird of the highest heavens and of the depths below; was it an expression of something in Manyosa that she dived into the water like this? Chikasa, that prosaic little fellow with the high-pitched voice, had given her a dull life. Here I was, trying out psychological explanations for her behavior, but there was more to it than that. I had learned to know Manyosa, with her St. Teresa-like flights of feeling and her abysmal despairs. There was a depth below, a passionate undersea where her feelings had to be submerged—literally, in that enamel bowl—to be drowned deep and to rise up. In my mind was the free call of the fish eagle as it raised itself after its dive, a sound that echoed over the forest. To the Ndembu this bird was the symbol of spirit itself. It was spirituality itself that was afflicting Manyosa and plunging her down.

I watched as my friend was led soaking and somber to the door of her house. Manyosa raised her eyes, gave me a gloomy greeting, and retired within.

The sight of Manyosa worried me. Next day I paid her a visit. Her face was heavy with agony.

"Manyosa! You ought to be in hospital. Look at you, Manyosa."

Mangaleshi came over to me and spoke in a low voice. "Manyosa is in seclusion, don't you see? The African doctors know she needs time for the spirit to do its work. There'll be another drum ritual soon, the Return-to-the-World ceremony."

In the women's chatting circle my urgency to get Manyosa off to hospital only bruised the group feeling.

"Nyamuvwila, too," I insisted. "You have to go to the leper sanitarium. You may be giving leprosy to the others here; please don't share their cups. Look, you're touching Chautongi. Don't." Nyamuvwila's eyes drew up; her mouth, full of projecting teeth, made a round shocked "Orh!" She stammered something and didn't talk to me for a long time.

I was as scared of leprosy as were the pharisees in the Bible. I knew it wasn't very dangerous, at least not to well-fed people; still, imagine drinking out of the same cup as a leper. Nyamuvwila seemed quite well, save that she was always rubbing a rough patch on her arm, rubbing with a bitter wry face, trying to bring the feeling back. I had come to see African skin as more lovely than polished wood, more potent and rich than chestnut buds. It felt as delicate as a deep tulip petal, and its dark surfaces ran with the complex play of muscles and tendons beneath. Often during our stay I was conscious of another beauty, the delicate interaction of the social body. Vic and I had been caught up in it, I knew. But in the late winter and sterile spring, that unity would not grow. A persistent rough patch disturbed us all. My diary was full of quarrels and law cases, countless half-fulfilled plans to improve the lot of the Ndembu, stories of our children's sickness and my spats with Vic, and complaints about the impossibility of pleasing everybody. The Africans had a peculiar brand of malice, we found; it would sometimes scald us and cripple us for days. We all needed a cure.

Manyosa's second Shaking ceremony took place several weeks later, near Nsimba's hut at night. When I arrived Nsimba was already in charge, deploying his personnel with a fine sense of organization. He still wore the long black coat with the astrakhan collar, and not one of us women could take our eyes off him.

Nsimba was a born impresario. He held Manyosa back for a special entrance; he organized an inner circle of doctors; to my surprise, a rattle was thrust into my hand and I was pushed forward to the stool next but one to Evita. I sat there feeling a little foolish, gripped for an instant with disbelief. But before the illusion broke altogether Nsimba, with the gestures of an old–time actor, took pieces of muteti bark and dealt them out to the doctors. I took mine. All together we put the chips into a large pot. Moving to the mortar, we all put our hands—many black and two white—on the pole and pounded the drinking medicine while the crowd sang and drummed. We were symbolizing our unity, a unity with the purpose of curing Manyosa, and I began to believe again.

Now Nsimba made us all take hold of the large pot and put it on the fire, after which a cup of beer was handed around. Now Manyosa was brought in, naked to the waist, looking depressed, yet somehow under the spell in spite of that. When she had been seated, old Kajima came forward. He bent down and prayed to his ancestors for Manyosa and for his people, dropping grains of white clay into the pot. Satisfied, he moved away and Nsimba took his place, praying into the pot, to which the spirit had been drawn by our collective actions.

He called into it like a priest into his chalice, his voice echoing: "Never mind, spirit, if we don't play the Ripening Drum or the Hunters' Drum for you; but look, we make Shaking Medicine for you." Anxiously, brusquely, he went on: "Come quick, quick." He fixed his eyes on the pot, watching the grains of chalk drifting on the surface of the water. His eyes grew crazy. He motioned in one direction as the chalk swung (toward Pond Village, a place of witchcraft? some wondered), and then in another direction (toward Samutamba Farm? thought others). This was divination. Nsimba looked up dramatically at us and swept the last piece of clay into the pot.

Then began the shaking, all around the circle, and then began the drums. Chikasa was standing apart, half supercilious about the whole business and half proud, in a circle of cronies. Further off stood a bunch of government clerks; the singing soothed them, and they joined in for a stanza or two, for few Africans could resist a drum ritual. Wandering around I found a log and rested awhile.

I could still see Nsimba's head within the circle, plunging up from the darkness. The crazy shiverers, Nsimba's pleased face with the astrakhan collar, the sinister dripping firelight, Manyosa's sulky look, the rattle still in my hand as I looked down, the well-known luscious music, my own companions sitting near—why all this? I sat on my log, gazing. My mind took me to a carpeted hotel bar back home. Two men in business suits stood handling glasses.

". . . down from the trees," one was saying. "It'll be two hundred years before they're literate."

Faintly I heard the other: ". . . religion? Sexual orgies all the time. Did you read *Lord of the Flies*? Shows you what happens to people separated from civilization. Unspeakable rites . . ."

The scene faded and resolved into the feel of naked black skin next to mine, shimmying warmly. Once again I heard Nsimba's gritty howl, hot with consciousness. I was quite at home. It all gave a sense of thick rich adult stew, oniony somehow; it was dirty as a zoo, savage as a boxing ring. Mr. Nsimba was drunk as a lord.

In sex it was the randyness that I liked—it was no good otherwise—and I found religion worked the same way: I liked the plunging and the possession much better than the contemplation of the holy. Why should religion be cold and good? Something in me said that sex and all the great creative acts bypassed reason and cold consciousness. The religious experience *came*, just like an African spirit.

Suddenly the village children were shouting and leaping around me. Samawika and Freddy had spent the afternoon making a little mask resembling Chizaluki, the Mad Chief. Samawika now thrust his face into the mask and came juntering forth, scraping and backing away, the very image of the circumcision spirit, until he arrived at the drums.

"Heh! Heh!" exclaimed the crowd and turned around, delighted. Samawika stopped dead from shyness. Musona pushed in front, grabbed the mask, and himself acted the gibing, gesturing figure, giving it a touch of the idiot. Everyone burst out laughing. People clambered out of the circle of shakers and pushed forward to watch Musona, so that Nsimba was left behind, looking weary and saddened in his funereal astrakhan. He glowered at the government clerks, who tittered.

Even the drummer had left his post, I noticed. I went over to him.

"Hey!" I said. "Don't leave the Shaking rite like this." He moved back. At that the whole crowd returned and reoccupied their places, and I took mine. Nsimba came over to me and shook my hand enthusiastically, then drew me into the dancing circle. This time I heard something new in the beat of the drums, a trip–hammer knock that sent my heart racing, a stutter that made me choke and grin, that set my heels tapping, my toes astretch. Every step ahead was a sway and a jerk; the drums took away effort and replaced it with a floating happiness. My chin seemed held up as if by a strong swimmer. As far as I was concerned, my feet never touched the ground.

Nsimba came near with a rattle and pressed the butt on my chest, a hollow tube of relief that took away everything that was evil inside me. I sighed and looked for my log seat; the short communion was over.

Late into the night the dance continued, until slowly what was only a gray stain on the night became light itself, then an enlarging of the whole world into the blue of day. The spirit of the spirit was now well washed into Manyosa with the medicine.

It was over. The scene was revealed in its humility, in a state of rest. Dead embers lay in a wide ring around the fire; sleeping children slept on. Nsimba and Evita were nowhere to be seen. I went up to the drummer, who was ruefully looking at his palms: they were bright red. Then my gaze fell on the leaf brushes that had been used for sprinkling and slapping Manyosa's body: to my horror the twigs were quite worn down. Manyosa moved from her place at last and struggled to her feet.

"Manyosa, are you all right?"

"I'm fine."

Her body looked bent and tired, but her eyes actually looked better. Nsimba now emerged from the bushes; he was in a sorry state, swaying about with bloodshot eyes. His hand went down, pointing for my benefit to a bandage that encircled his leg. There was a nasty gash where the bandage sagged. Nsimba looked up from it.

"Stabbed," he groaned. "Er, that is to say . . . I tripped up on some pointed firewood. It . . . stabbed me."

At the same moment Evita stumbled toward me with her skirt hauled up. She showed me a savage cut high up on her leg next to her privates. I winced.

"What on earth have you been doing?"

"What are you talking about? I stumbled on a hoe set up the wrong way in the dark. Give me a plaster, will you?"

(Eh, come on, you two. So you don't dare to admit you were fighting? Everyone knows you are jealous of each other's affairs at night.)

"Sure, I'll fetch one." I fixed up the embarrassing wound with salve and bandaids, then did the same for Nsimba.

"You guys will have to look out for yourselves," I said. The two looked at each other and grinned. I stared and shook my head.

Nsimba was anxious about another matter. It appeared he worked as a builder at the government center, five miles away.

It was now half past eight, long after his starting time. He looked like a condemned man.

"Would you," he begged, "give me a letter saying I've had an accident? Otherwise they'll sack me." Both his hands were holding his head together.

"Who should I write to?" I asked, trying to find my notebook. I wasn't feeling very alert myself.

"To the Tutolika." (This was the plural of Katolika, "Catholic.") Nsimba's face grew sentimental. "Good people." Nsimba, then, was building the church for the missionaries near the market.

"I'll fix it," I said, more confused still. Would the religions ever be able to understand each other? And yet at Nsimba's level, why, they could!

Manyosa was pitifully warm and happy now, since the rites could go on and Nsimba's presence was assured.

After a short break the participants gathered in a business-like way for the next stage. Manyosa came over to talk to me; she was looking more of a person than before.

"I'll explain what is going to happen," she said, leading me into the bush with the others to arrange the new rites. Her face was excited and a little furtive.

"I'm to be a diviner," she explained, speaking low. I could hardly hear, so I put my head closer. "You may watch, as you are on the way to being a doctor yourself. We saw the spirit catch you in the dance." I frowned, then remembered being held up as if by a powerful swimmer. "You will see me guess the hiding place of four things," and she struck them off on her fingers. "A shilling, some beads, a comb, and a needle. This power of guessing is wonderful."

I overtook Nsimba and Evita, who had stopped by the bole of a very tall ironwood tree. Their choice was determined by its height and strength, for beneath its shade a patient might overcome even the worst, the "tallest" diseases, the European ones, that emanated from high society.

Evita was busy hoeing a large mound of soil. Muttering and conferring, she and Nsimba shaped it into a large animal with a head, body, tail, and four legs—a lion. Satisfied with their work, they looked around cautiously. Manyosa had gone away. They took the four objects, the shilling, beads, comb, and needle, and hid them here and there under the earthy body of the lion. Then they patted the soil back into place. They grinned at me and nudged in the direction of the absent Manyosa. Nsimba doubled over in soundless mirth at the absurdity of the thing; his hangover was forgotten.

Then Manyosa descended like a lion between me and Evita, elbowing past our crouched forms. I moved quickly aside as Manyosa straddled the animal, lion to lion, and swept her hand through its body, upturning with one stroke the comb, beads, and needle. Then, pouting with concentration, she *divined,* and her hand fell like a hawk on the hidden shilling. They all jumped up and hooted, and immediately went dancing with a honky-tonk tune back to the village. I took the opportunity to drift away and devour some breakfast.

Just as I started to stir my tea I heard Musona glide in behind me. He went to the cutlery box. "Is it all right to take a knife and fork for the European Dinner?" he asked. He apparently knew the answer because he was helping himself. He lifted up a folded tablecloth and looked at it.

I was still sleepy from the night before and couldn't make out what he was talking about. Then I remembered. At the end of the Shaking ceremony the patient becomes a European for a time and the spirit demands European food. Musona was the obvious person to collect the props. I said, "You'll want some tea and sugar as well, won't you? Yes, take that tablecloth."

I hurriedly finished my breakfast and went along to the village. Here came Manyosa with her entourage, firm and grave of face, already advancing across the plaza like a visiting ambassador. She turned when she reached our umbrella tent and entered it, our poor old tent, gaunt and neglected. I walked past the tent, as if I just happened to be going that way, and shot a look inside. Manyosa was seated, with a royal straight back, remote and grand at a small camp table, which was covered with our tablecloth. Kandaleya hovered over her, dressed in an immaculate maid's uniform, borrowed from the tramp daughter-in-law who worked at the Protestant mission. Kandaleya was feeding Manyosa seriously, feeding her plain rice, tucking it into her mouth with a fork. As I moved to see better, I nearly bumped into another waiter, coming along with tea in a glass. He advanced with a genteel posture, the glass elegantly held up at his shoulder. He offered it to Manyosa with his little finger cocked. Nobody laughed. It was strikingly different from the way a present is given to a headman, when both hands are used as with a chalice, a different but also superb politeness.

The waiter frowned at me and the faces around looked shocked. "Europeans do not like being watched while they are eating," growled the waiter. The turnabout was dizzying me. I was no longer European, Manyosa was. The game was serious.

Later Manyosa emerged, willowy, almost beautiful in her long robe; she circled the tent accompanied by her train, and then retired for her afternoon nap, in the manner of Europeans.

The next morning I happened to be sitting in the children's sleeping hut stitching Freddy's camp cot, which had been torn when he had bounced clean through it the night before. I shoved the needle in with the inane patience of a woman who actually likes monotonous work, for my mind was elsewhere. It was the right moment for a shy figure to appear at the door, accompanied by a delicious scent.

"Manyosa!"

She was wonderfully dressed up, with beads on her head, at her neck, her waist, and a gay smile, a new headcloth, and I could swear she had curled her eyelashes and plucked her eyebrows. She shimmered in and grasped my hand, smiling like the open sun into my eyes.

"My dear, I am cured!" she trilled, and sat down gracefully.

Actually cured? The goiter did look smaller.

"Ah, the Shaking drum, it is so beautiful. It was all true, what they told me. A spirit did come, and it helped me find the four objects. It pushed my hand, I felt it; it was a marvel."

Manyosa's greatness had come. She sat filled with the spirit: diviner, traveler into the hearts of the Europeans, conqueror of her own bad dreams. She had struggled, been patient, and had been rewarded with a moment of beauty and vision, crowned with the solemn rite of the Dinner, a rite far beyond chieftainship, deep in the remote world of Englishmen; the Dinner, served with religious cleanliness and control, tense with reverence. I remembered that world now, sitting on the bed by Manyosa. Yes, I once stood in their deep perfect houses, Manyosa: the dean's house at Ely, the provost's house at Coventry, and the houses of great cultured ladies at Aldeburgh. That air of quiet, with the rich immortal arts set in leather bindings, rubied in cabinets, dim in grand pianos—it held a solemnity and magic past anything seen in this dull world of today.

What has become of that awe? I dared not inquire, in case I should find it had gone forever. Have the Catholics cornered it and then squandered it? Has the secret been stolen by the Russians and has it melted away in their hands?

No, it has been turned into tears. We couldn't believe in it any more, so now all we have left are tears when we feel a drift of it passing, tears of fear and happiness and mourning, still hoping that God might love us, might love our huge altogether shabby world, perhaps because it's funny, or some such reason.

I faced Manyosa straight, seeing helplessly through her eyes, and the spell slowly opened out and let me in. How can I learn to speak about those things of which one cannot speak?

Shaking, possession, and trance take place up and down the continent of Africa, out in the black Americas, and all over the nontheological world. They start with submission and the loss of self; then in an unexpected moment comes the arrival of the spirit, in great happiness and freedom; afterwards come the two gifts, which are clairvoyance, such as Manyosa experienced, and healing. There is a direct continuum from this Shaking rite to Voodoo and to Umbanda and Candomblé in Brazil. More generally, the same glory is experienced by the Juggernaut devotee gazing into the saucer eyes of the image, becoming possessed as the huge tower that bears it is heaved along in procession; it is authentically related to the delight of the Pentecostals and charismatics when the spirit thrills them, and to the Quakers' joy in the old days. The same is found in the Balinese dancer gone from ecstasy into trance as his strange hands curve and point; is heard from the throat of the white clarinetist in the midst of the jazz band, pouring it all out; is seen in the great actor suddenly possessed by his role, in flow, a state he finds hard to remember afterwards; in the Hasids' circling arm in arm on the roof of their shrine, in trance all night; in the medieval Christian mystic's trance; and in the saint's humble prayer for the sick man before him, vaguely aware that God is flowing through him to the sufferer, who rises cured, wearing a smile of wonder. The neurobiologists understand the internal spillover effect, but they still have work to do explaining the miracles. As for Manyosa, she was alive again, her despair was cured, and she was ready to go away for her physical cure.

Everyone agreed that it was time she went. The only one in ignorance of her careful preparation was the white surgeon in the mining town. How was he to realize that the courage he confronted was the result of the efforts of a whole village?

Still, Manyosa's difficulties were many; even making the first arrangements was hard enough. I sent her to the local government clinic with a letter, asking them to send her to the copperbelt hospital where they were equipped to remove the goiter. Another goiter sufferer, Sakazao's slave wife Nyakalusa, decided to go for the operation, too. Together they walked the five miles to Mwinilunga, finding themselves at the District Office. Sick, with bare feet on the red polished floor, they approached the desk.

"No admittance, no admittance!" shouted the black clerk.

They tried again the next day, wandering from office to office. At length they were directed to a building that was the tiniest of pillboxes; it was the government clinic. They put their noses in at the door and goggled, observing a single row of medicine bottles. "Off!" shouted the medical orderly. "The clinic is only open Thursdays. Out you get, you stupid bush natives."

They went on Thursday with a rewritten letter from me, piteous enough to melt the heart of a prison jailer. On Friday, while I sat writing fieldnotes, Chautongi came by.

"Manyosa's back," she threw out casually.

I jumped to my feet. "Back? Why?" Frightfully full of anger I stalked through the village, to find Manyosa sitting in her kitchen, looking at loose ends.

"Greetings. What did the orderly say?"

Manyosa sighed. "Mishy, he said: you must first write a letter to the mission station"—fifty miles in the other direction—"and the doctor there must give Transporti a letter next week on Thursday, and I must be ready on that day." Transporti was The Northern Transport Company Omnibus, the huge slat-seated rickety old bus-cum-mailvan-cum-freighter that plied once a week from town to Mwinilunga District and back again.

"Oh," I sighed. There would be no mail to the mission until the following Thursday. When the time came I wrote, my eloquence almost spent. Nothing happened. Thursdays came and went, and I forgot the matter. One morning it occurred to me to ask, "Where's Manyosa?"

"Manyosa?" said Chautongi. "Oh, yes, she and Nyakalusa left last Thursday."

"Are they doing all right? Any news?"

"A message came through from the clinic. They're being sent through to the miners' hospital in town." I closed my eyes.

News of a vague kind came about them. They were to stay a month, then six weeks. We were busy, as always. It must have been about seven weeks later that the usual Thursday Transporti, instead of stopping briefly on its way to the north to drop off Vic's mail, roared closer and plunged unexpectedly into the ancient Kajima footpath, now reverting to bush. On it came, beating down young shrubs, all the way into the village. It stopped by the chota, the back opened, and out tottered Manyosa and Nyakalusa.

"Yey-ey-ey!" The village gathered like fans around film stars. I ran forward to greet them; both necks were encircled with stiff white bandages.

"Welcome back!" I cried, then stopped, as Manyosa raised her head painfully. I restrained my impulse to slap her on the back, and instead took her hand as flabbily as she took mine, grateful for her exhausted recognition. "Poor old girl," I thought.

Now the women all around brought their hands up and together in a swooping motion and burst out singing, escorting the returning pair to seats beside the chota. "Ey, yey-yey. Momma we prayed, yey, yey, yey." The faces of Manyosa and Nyakalusa showed no sign of feeling and I respected the convention this time, looking with awe at their control.

As the crowd gathered by the chota, Chikasa appeared in the middle of it flourishing his musket. He brought it to his shoulder, pointed it to the sky, and fired. Manyosa jerked, the corners of her lips twitching. A gun salute! And into the circle came Master Kajima to give his welcome. "You have reached home," he pronounced in the traditional words. "We kept your yard swept clear of familiars while you were away. We were thinking of you." This sweeping was the Ndembu metaphor for prayer.

Manyosa sat stiffly on her stool, bowed a little forward. There was a gracious touch to her tiredness, but she was still silent.

"Go lie down," I said. "I can see you're not feeling good." But Manyosa insisted on staying until the songs were ended.

Late that night I was awakened by a rustling at my grass door. Vic was away, so the hut seemed sad and quiet. I lit a candle and went to the opening; Musona's face looked in on me. It was anxious.

"Mishy, come with me, please," he said. "Manyosa is very ill. The jogging of Transporti has made her big wound bad."

I staggered out sleepily. At the back of my mind rose my own post-operation misery six years before. "If the stitches will only hold," I thought, while looking for a clean bandage. Hard, though, when you're sure they're going to give way; after all, the familiar flesh has been raped open. I grabbed some aspirin, and decided to take some antiseptic in case the wound was in a bad state. I made my way along to Manyosa's hut, treading in my thin sandals over the cool sands of the plaza. Chautongi was sitting inside the hut tending a kerosene lamp. This was the first time I had entered; the door, that paneled door set in the dull expanse of wall, had always stood shut, as if Manyosa wanted to hide the nights Chikasa was home. Manyosa sat on the side of her bed, holding her arms up against the wall as if she were keeping the mud plaster in place. Was this posture helping her to keep the stitches together?

She put out a hand and clutched my dress. "I am dying," she said, looking up to the rafters. Her strong upward gaze left her lower eyelids behind like lost children. One hand tried to gesture sensibly, but it seemed that even moving her fingers hurt. What a fit of nerves! Back again flew my memory to my operation, when I'd had those awful nerves myself.

I took Manyosa by the hand. "Come and sleep in my hut tonight, and I'll give you medicine and make sure you're all right. I won't let you die."

Manyosa wavered upright and came along. I led her across to

my hut and laid her on my camp cot, with pillows behind the painful neck. Then I made a really strong cup of tea with sugar in it and fed it to her with a teaspoon, my own version of the European Dinner. I gave her three aspirins and plenty of tender care. Long she lay back on the pillows and talked, with a weak little voice and a mouth that hardly moved.

"They cut my throat, they cut it through. Orgh, I shall never be all right now."

Later: "The copperbelt, it's a terrible place, Mishy. The food was exceedingly bad. They forced us to eat beef, those hard little lumps of beef. No antelope, no cassava, Mishy; they even forced us to eat corn meal." Manyosa's teeth were on edge at the memory of the gritty concoction.

"While I was asleep they cut my throat. And I had this dream. Mwendiana came into the hospital hut; you've heard of Mwendiana, my sister who died young—ey, she was beautiful; she had traveled in many countries, being married to a clever Malawi boy. And she was the one who could not live. But she came back from the dead that day in the hospital. She leaned over me and looked into my open throat. Then she said, 'Nessy my daughter is coming to see you.' Mishy, you know what? The very next day Nessy came."

The warmth of this miraculous visitation ran through both of us. Was Mwendiana perhaps with us now? Soon Manyosa began to talk more naturally. "No, really," she went on. "The journey back was the trouble. That motor bus is not good for sick people, it jogs. It was a very awful journey." I knew it was, even on the sprung cushions in the cab of our truck.

I caressed her, and found her sitting up the next moment. She wanted to go home.

"Do you think you could? It's true, you'd sleep better at home." Manyosa managed the walk back, holding onto my arm.

Returning to my lonely hut, I lay down on the bed and slept soundly.

"Yecch—the beef! Lumps of wood! You wouldn't believe it.

The copperbelt, my dear! Awful. Corn meal, I mean to say, *corn* meal. Pebbles in it. Can you credit it? The bus? Jog-a-jog-jog, sudden death!" Her staccato phrases tapped out wherever her friends gathered. For weeks the village delighted in her disgust.

Manyosa was my mother, sister, and daughter, and she was grandmother to little Rene. Her pinched-up eyes and goggling gaze, full of pity and emotion, remained in my mind for years to come. So often I had looked into her eyes and squeezed the thumb of her hand, feeling the worldly gaiety of this friend of mine as we shared the same stool (Manyosa was so thin that this was possible). The thread of friendship held; we were both conscious persons, knowing it couldn't last, both sad seeing each other's eyes sad, thinking of the future. I knew I had become trapped and rooted in real existence here in Africa. And it meant loss. Manyosa had been the one to root me, Manyosa, whom I was going to lose.

THE SORCERER'S RAGE

HOW CAN I DRAW with one firm line the picture of my African year? The curve of events draws my narrative forward and takes me some time into the future. Then I must lift the pencil and go back to gather what was left behind and bring that forward, always tracing more of the complex shape of social life in time. Thus the shadowy sketch emerges: not the picture of a flat finite object, but of something composite, made up of the stories of many individual wills, full of stray ends, like hair which yet may glisten when brushed and sunned.

Samutamba was in a good position on the Kajima genealogy. He was matrilineal first cousin once removed of the headman, and was married to Nyamuvwila's daughter Engeniya, a round-faced Malabu. Samutamba himself was a long-face with pinchy eyes, a sardonic version of the Nyachintangas. His troubles arose from the natural vitality of his character. As often happens in such cases, his style of living was frowned upon and labeled sin and sorcery. Nevertheless he was an able man, and his very ability was to blame for the bitter feeling in the village.

Before we arrived in Kajima, Musona and Manyosa lived in the warm presence of their mother, whose name Nyamwaha,

"Good Mother," told all. She was the matriarch of the village, sister to Master Kajima, and also acted as the mother of Samutamba. She was a tall fine old lady, with crinkly hair that was almost white and a face that was long and folded and very wrinkled between the eyes. Those eyes were a little rheumy with age, but they darted keenly when her grandchildren crawled helter-skelter in and out of her kitchen. She herself looked after her granddaughter's milk tree rites. Musona was often away, but Manyosa acquired more of her mother's character with every day that passed. Samutamba worked nearby on the government road. His own mother was dead and he was glad to receive Nyamwaha's frequent dishes of cassava. At the same time he experienced twinges of jealousy for her real children; he was sure she cheated him out of a dish of beans when she fed the others.

As for Engeniya, she should have been a strong link binding Samutamba to Kajima Village. Engeniya loved to visit with her mother and cousins and tell stories of town.

"Engeniya," her cousins asked her. "Show us how they wear their evening dresses at the governor's ball." Engeniya took a dress length of red cloth and wrapped it around her body under the armpits. She tucked it in tightly. Then she swept about for a minute, holding her head high; from the top of her braided head to her sloping shoulders and down to her feet she was magnificent.

Chautongi the mission convert approached, carrying a basket. "Eh! There's Engeniya with her shoulders naked. Is that how Samutamba likes his women?"

Engeniya's face glittered with wrath. She took off the cloth, folded it, and stalked away.

There was a great deal wrong with Engeniya's marriage and everybody knew it. To make it worse, Samutamba began to drink. One day when he was far gone the merest trifle set the two to quarreling.

"Engeniya!" he shouted. "I told yer before. Why didn'tcher

brew sheven calabashes beer? There's this . . . this Guinea Fowl shelebration coming up . . ."

"Guinea Fowl dance? Not Guinea Fowl. You're drunk, Samutamba. Didn't you know it was a Ripening ceremony? Two calabashes is quite enough."

"You telling me, gal? Go do what I order you." Seeing her expression of loathing, he picked up a stick. Nsimba, who was passing outside, heard her screaming and rushed in. He grabbed the stick from the drunken man.

Samutamba had some particularly painful home truths ready for Nsimba.

"Nsimba, stink cat. Livin' off yer wife's tail. After my wife now! Stink cat. Shit in little turds under a tree. Gedout!" Samutamba swayed toward the dodging pimp with some more ideas. "I seen what's under yer pants: balloon balls, swollen up with pus."

Nsimba involuntarily looked down at his pants. Samutamba caught him a blow to drive him out of the door, which filled Nsimba with choking fury. He smashed Samutamba against the wall, crushing his elbow savagely, then, seeing blood, he turned and ran.

Samutamba staggered to the door, clutching his elbow. Okay, he would leave: he had intended to for a long time. He plunged out, making for his kitchen to find food for the journey, being careful to include a couple of goats' horns stoppered with wax—his medicines, connected with a certain private ritual he was performing to insure his own success and the downfall of his enemies. Before he left he would say goodbye to Nyamwaha, but there was no sign of her. That affected him badly and he shook with sobs, never noticing that he had dropped one of the horns on the dirt floor of Nyamwaha's kitchen. He scrabbled his money out of a hole in the ground, then started out, walking up his own road to the northern capital.

The weather had been heavy when Nyamwaha started on her chores earlier that morning. She looked about in her kitchen and saw that the meal basket was empty. She would have to undertake the long round of digging, soaking, carrying, exchanging wet and dry cassava, pounding, and sifting. She sighed. Still, it was worth it; she liked to feed Samutamba, of whom she was rather fond.

She was tired, but once she was down in the fields the old muscles responded to the task of hoeing up the roots. She worked a little jerkily because her hip hurt. She experienced one severe pain when she lifted the full basket to her head; then it was easier because the path led downhill to the river. Still, the weather didn't look good. She exchanged wet and dry roots in the soaking pool, and as she lifted up the load of soggy cassava to her head drops of rain fell. Her already dry cassava at home would get wet.

The old lady started to hurry up the steep path. She had never yet put down a basket to rest, and she wasn't going to now. The rain stopped, but her mind was locked into a panic of haste. Arriving at the village, she took the whole mat of dried cassava in under her thatch, then looked out. Still no storm. The mortar stood handy, so she fetched the pole and filled the big wooden vase, inadvertently treading on a goat's horn on the ground. She started to pound. Chunk! An agony shot from her chest into her shoulder, into the pole, into the kitchen post she clutched, and down into the ground as she fell, where the pain seemed to spread into the whole world. The black was sudden and total.

Hearing the thump and the clatter of the falling pole, Manyosa rushed up.

"Momma, Momma! Yey, grief, grief. What's happened? Darling Momma. Yey-yey-yey!"

Chautongi tiptoed up, solemn and awful; she bent to look and pronounced, "She is dead." Lifting up her head for a moment she might have been praying, and for an instant she had dignity. But then she remembered something.

"In this kitchen, earlier, I saw him. You know who I mean. He placed bad medicine for Nyamwaha, making sorcery. He's done this to take his revenge on the village."

Manyosa turned eyes full of violence toward Samutamba's house. "That's it. Ey, Momma, Momma!"

Master Kajima was now beside them, his face like black marble. It was his own sister. He could not cry or speak yet, not until the ritual of mourning began.

The village forbade any attempt by Samutamba to return during the year that followed. What was in his mind no one knew, and nothing was worse in the eyes of the villagers than the hidden mind. Later, Engeniya visited him in his northern retreat. When they met, to the surprise of both, they found themselves weeping together, for they had loved their good mother, Nyamwaha.

A week later they returned together to Kajima, where the familiar bushes at the entrance brought them to the point of tears again. For Samutamba it was still the Kajima of Nyamwaha's living presence. The people gathered, the memory of Nyamwaha reviving in their minds, and as the crowd went forward to enclose them Chautongi's scandal faded. Wailing arose as if the funeral had begun once more.

Kajima approached with tears running down his cheeks, wailing again for his sister. His eyes searched Samutamba's face and he saw how like Nyamwaha he was. Samutamba, weeping, voiced the funeral song between sobs.

"Samutamba," said Kajima. "You have reached home."

"Let us make a shrine," said Samutamba, standing among them with his head back. "Let us plant a tear tree for Nyamwaha and let her daughter Manyosa take over her name." And so it was. They brought drums, and placed the daughter Manyosa and her cousin Samutamba before the village shrine trees, marking the pair with white clay on the temples. They brought a thick stubby length of wood with no roots, wet at each end where the sap ran clear, a kind that would root itself in the earth and grow; drumming and singing, they planted the tree, using the butts of their ritual rattles. At the climax, after pouring white beer at the foot of the new tree for Nyamwaha, they named Manyosa Swana-Nyamwaha, "Inheritor of Good Mother," and everyone sighed with relief. Later, when the leaves of the tear tree sprouted, they knew Nyamwaha was there in it. They could see Samutamba and Manyosa seated around it in white clothes amid the blending voices of the villagers.

Samutamba was Vic's special friend. He had the knack of arriving with a teapot full of millet beer whenever fieldwork became a headache to Vic, or a problem seemed insurmountable. It was uncanny how Samutamba knew when he was needed. I can see his Humphrey Bogart smile now, and the white teapot. The two men would sit together on proper chairs at our table and pour out the brew. The small holes designed to keep the tea leaves from going into the cup also served to hold back the millet grains, providing the men with a perfect cup. After those delicate drafts of milky alcohol and some worldly grumbling on both sides, Vic would feel just fine.

Samutamba varied one of these occasions by inviting us to his own house. It was late in the evening; having groped around the paths to the side of the house, we had to feel our way in the darkness to find the corner of the wall. Along the further wall we were conscious of high windows set in the brick, and for some reason I imagined a second row of windows above them— a baronial two-floor house—but of course there were none. The paneled portal in the center opened to us, and we were ushered in by Engeniya, appearing in the darkness like a statue of quietness in her red robe. We found ourselves in an echoing hall whose walls seemed made of ancient stone. Engeniya conducted us to a room on the right, from which glowed the light of a hurricane lamp. We sat down by the calabashes on handsomely carved stools and raised our heads to receive the greetings of Samutamba's guests, government employees and growers of cash crops from beside the road. They were in a cheerful mood, for there was honey mead in the calabashes. Even I waxed witty that evening, as far as I can remember, and they were rather nice to me. The next thing I remember was walking back across the village later, arm in arm with Vic, looking up at the full moon and feeling remarkably optimistic, so much so that when I arrived at the hut I did what I had always wanted to do: I bounced down on the camp bed so that it tilted up and deposited me neatly in the narrow space between it and the grass wall behind. That was fun. I lay looking up and giggling. I gather Vic thought I was drunk.

On one such occasion, after Samutamba had spent an evening with his friends, he pulled Engeniya down onto the bed with him. She wriggled delightedly as paroxysms of feeling overwhelmed her. His plunges were so welcome, so welcome. Afterwards, her hand came up to wipe the semen onto her breast, an act of wifely piety.

"Eh! That again!" she exclaimed. Her hand was slimy with a dark evil fluid. "Red semen—red semen. You know you really are a sorcerer, Samutamba."

He jerked up, giddy and furious. "You Kajima women!" he roared. "Sly, pious Malabu types!" He fell on her and wrenched her arm back, crashing his arm across her nose.

"Yee, yee, yee!" she screamed, her nose running with blood. She snatched her robe and twirled it around her breast. Dodging another onslaught, she skipped around the corner and ran sobbing from the house.

Samutamba looked at his woolly crotch and smeared penis. All his passion and bitterness rose in one roar. He grabbed his pants, weeping as he missed the leg hole, made it the second time, and ran to the door. He knew where Engeniya had gone and followed her. Mad with rage and alcohol he penetrated the darkness around the outside paths of Kajima, and thence to the purlieus of Nyamuvwila's hut, where Engeniya and her mother sat huddled together. His wavering terrible step ceased at the hut, and he began to shout—at his sly mother-in-law, at his colorless brothers-in-law, at his pious and over-fertile father-in-law, at his odious rival Nsimba, and, worst of all, his shrewish wife Engeniya. Chautongi, Manyosa, Mangaleshi, and Mesala came out of their huts and stood by their doors, watching.

"Wa-anza we-eyi!" went the crazed voice. "Dirt in your foreskin!"

Mesala tittered somewhere, from a safe distance; Manyosa muttered ironically and withdrew. No one dared quieten him, least of all those who were the targets of his wrath. Sporadically, like the thunder, the voice raged on all night.

"Wa-anza we-eyi!"

Away in our camp Vic and I heard the long-drawn-out curse. We too crept out of doors and stood listening.

DRUMS OF THE THUNDER

THE RAIN CAME AT LAST. In the village the small boys were running naked through it, shouting "Nvula-a!" The grown-ups came to their hut doors and gazed out marveling and fond, and all smelled the fresh sweet heavenly scent of the wet earth.

Hadn't the dry season been summer? A summer of drought? I had wandered so long in the tired bush and the long stretches of yellow grass that I had begun to expect autumn, and finally winter. It was true, the start of the dry "summer" was the encroachment of the desert summer from the paler regions of the subtropics—a time of sterility, dust, and tropical ulcers. Why Englishwomen in Africa preferred the dry season I did not know. Did they fear what was likely to follow?

What the weeks now led us into was beyond the range of all the seasons I had known. If we had already been through summer, what was this? Instead of swinging back into winter, the world seemed to run forward, first into a region of fire and then deep into a tumult of thunderstorms. The thatch of our grass huts became sodden, and I constantly felt drips of water down my neck when I sat writing. This needed some hard thinking. I found the large tarpaulin that had come with the umbrella tent and spread it out. As I feared, most of it had worn thin where we had trodden on it, leaving a cottony open weave. This would not help our roof. I had in mind the possibility of using bees-wax—a product available locally in large balls the size of mel-ons, sold by hunters—as waterproofing. Itota the hunter had some on hand; I took a ball home, feeling the hardness of the lump on the way. It was too hard: I needed to soften the wax so that I could paint it on the tarpaulin. I tried placing the ball in a bucket of gasoline, but nothing happened. The wax clearly needed heat, so I brought a tub of boiling water from the kitchen and placed the bucket in it. Sure enough, after a time the wax oiled considerably. I put my hands in it to divide the lump and meld it with the stinging gasoline. At last it was ready, a soft oily cream, smelling like extra fierce floor polish. Freddy and I spread out the tarpaulin and slopped the wax all over it until the thin weave was sealed up. Then the greasy canvas had to be hauled up onto the roof, maneuvered into place, and roped down. We watched eagerly in the next storm and saw the wax ball up the raindrops and send them hurtling down off the roof into the drainage ditch that ran all around the hut. The thatch soon dried inside, the photographic film survived, the type-writer worked, and the books opened. The umbrella tent itself provided the same protection for the children's hut.

The unearthly season developed. Every afternoon at four, convection currents boiled up from the land. I visualized the furred forested floor of a great kettle, from which thousands of bubbles ascended to the skies on a geographic scale. Outside our hut the familiar masses closed over the trees in a black roof, and in a moment—crash!—the storm started. It never finished until we were all nerveshaken one way or another—by a crack a few feet over our heads, by an appalling explosion as a thun-derball burst in a garden nearby, by a prolonged display of light-ning all around us in a circle, or by the sight of the water rushing past our door in defiance of our drainage ditches. Chasmal gray waterfalls seemed to hang perpetually between us and the vil-lage; women crept about between storms, chilled in their soaked cottons, some of them developing the hangdog expression that signifies malaria; I myself knew that cold feeling. Many of the villagers were worrying about their cassava plants in the gardens, bowed down under the storm. The women wondered if they had made the mounds high enough to give the roots drainage, or would rot set in?

At night Vic read stories to the children as we squatted on the edges of the camp cots, which we had pulled away from the wall posts for fear the posts might conduct lightning. Beyond the thatch, and above the roofs of every house in the village, rode "Our Grandfather," the god of the thunder, a difficult curmudgeon of a spirit, the greatest of the afflictors and the greatest of the allies. His was the drenching rain that enclosed us all, that in an unexpected way overarched our troubles and comforted us, making us feel cozy and cared for.

At the same time, sickness was rife in Kajima and its neighborhood. Masondi suffered a severe burn on her shin, which became infected and would take months to heal in this climate, even with my constant attention. The local bully, a former mine policeman, picked a quarrel with Samutamba and nearly murdered him. Rosina caught pneumonia, which, to my surprise, I was able to cure with the application of a kaolin poultice. Four babies in the neighborhood caught bronchitis; in every case I took the mother and baby on the carrier of my bicycle up hill and down dale to the clinic so that the baby could have a shot, but each time the disease had obtained too strong a hold and the baby died. I began to feel hollow. The husbands of Mesala and Chautongi both appeared to have the symptoms of sickle cell disease. Rosina's baby began to show disturbing signs of malignant malnutrition; her hair grew reddish and sparse, and she looked dull. Worst of all, Nyamuvwila's leprosy was advancing.

Nyamuvwila suffered in many ways. She carried on with her work, digging, soaking, carrying, pounding, and cooking. To and fro she trudged on the long pathways; at least she saw that Master Kajima was fed. But her mind churned. Her daughter

Engeniya would never have children, and her other daughter was lost to her in town. Although Kajima was her home, she was lonely. Her sons were dull company.

"What did I get out of marrying this headman?" she complained. "Eh, this arm, this numbness." She rubbed in vain; the feeling would not return. And Engeniya would never give birth.

The rain spattered before Nyamuvwila's feet as she struggled back home with her basket; the path became slippery and her body had to be as stiff as a ramrod under the heavy load. She thought of the coming night. She would be sleepless again in that damp hut amid the mosquitoes. Who could keep well? Evening sent nasty little beings under her door. Was her hut full of leprosy like that entire village of leaf eaters she had heard about? She would never be able to persuade her old man to build a new hut. She thought pathetically, wretchedly, of Teresa, her daughter in town, a lovely woman who combined Manyosa's strong nature with a beauty that surpassed Engeniya's. Town was so far away. In despair she set down her basket, ran into the bush, and flung herself down sobbing.

"I shall die, I shall die. I shall rot like the awful cripple boy of the leaf eaters. My children are done for. Eh, babies, babies."

The night before she had dreamed that she had just given birth to a new baby of her own, but she had no milk in her breasts. It was because there was no nourishment in her food, because there was no meat. Remembering the dream now she seemed to go mad. Trembling, she saw little men staring at her mockingly from between the trees. Then came the horror of death.

As she lay facing the ground she heard something plop down by her ear. It was a fresh pear from some tree above. She fingered its soft surface and eventually took a bite of it. "That nutty taste," she said to herself. All around the pears lay thick, interspersed with antelope footprints; this would be good news for Kajima.

The pears and the footprints, backed by a distant roll of thunder, were telling her something. The deep bush in the rains—there was a power down there much bigger than her pothers about Teresa and Engeniya; it was very healthy, it was wild and exciting. She looked at the pear tree and for a moment saw a great whiteness everywhere; it was not mere lightning, because it gave her a feeling of comfort, as if she had just eaten a good meal.

Puzzled, she went back for her basket. Then she thought, "Of course there's something we can do: go to a diviner. This is a matter for those who can tell the Pieces of Perception."

It had been a long journey. The small party stood in a field outside a village on the border of Angola. Divining was illegal, which meant that diviners felt more at ease where an international boundary lay close by, to provide an escape route.

In the distance Nyamuvwila and Kajima could see a crude gateway consisting of a couple of upright poles and a high crosspiece; as they watched, two figures—a solitary man followed by a young boy—made their way under it and came toward them. The man wore a respectable fedora on his head, and at his waist a leopard skin, an eyecatching object. As they approached, Nyamuvwila caught sight of the baskets held by the assistant; one was a square-patterned storage basket with a beautifully fitting lid and the other was open, a flat winnowing basket to winnow the truth from lies. The diviner entered the circle of Kajima villagers, and with one accord the party sat down. They looked at his brown eyes and saw how they swam with uncertainty, and they wondered. The winnowing basket was ready before him, filled with the Pieces of Perception. There were the Family (mother, child, and father), the Hypocrite, the Tale Bearer, the Knotted Hide (representing the twisted mind), the Phallus, the Mirror, the Mountain (representing a weighty matter), Frozen Tears, the Funeral Fires (a stick burnt in notches), the Hyena, the Coin, the Set of Calabashes (three shards on a string, representing marriage), and the Ancient Nut of Time. As the diviner grasped the basket, they noticed that his index finger and fourth finger were missing; he was maimed. No one realized that it was the unquenched heat vibrations at the place of the missing digits that directed the shaking of the basket. It was an old technique among some African diviners.

The diviner tossed; the carved brown figures jostled in the air and fell. Most obvious were the Family, the Tale Bearer with her huddled arms, and near her the Knotted Hide. The Set of Calabashes protruded a little from underneath. Nyamuvwila peeped into the basket. Was she going to be accused of being a tale bearer again?

"You married into a hostile family, did you not, Nyamuvwila?" Nyamuvwila looked puzzled. The Nyachintangas had often attacked her, but she had always thought she was in the wrong.

"Why, yes, they are. Hostile."

He lifted the basket and tossed again, causing the Pieces to rattle against each other. When they came to rest the Calabashes had disappeared; now the Family stood out with the Hyena lying across the Child in the middle. But tilted over them both lay the Nut of Time.

"So. It's not just you, is it, Nyamuvwila?" His voice wheezed at every breath. "Look, the Child. The Child lies beneath the Sorcerer."

"Engeniya, why yes." Nyamuvwila's eyes filled with tears. "She cannot give me grandchildren."

"Look at the Nut of Time." The diviner's voice was shaken with asthmatic coughing. In the midst of it he seemed to grasp something and come to himself.

"The Nut from Long Ago. You must seek the Old Grandfather. I will not name him. Seek him in the bush; but enter his domain little by little, or you will anger him."

And he would say no more.

They paid him and turned for home; Nyamuvwila was tired,

but a new hope was in her. When they were nearing the village Kajima said suddenly: "The Grandfather may be called forth with Chihamba, the Shit ritual."

"What's that? Eh, I remember," and she smiled at the name, recalling a ceremony whose novices had been known to defecate like babies in the presence of the Grandfather. "Okay, we'll do it." She began to plan. "We'll brew seven calabashes of our own; Engeniya can do another seven. Manyosa will help, of course. Who'll officiate?"

They fell to thinking. Apart from the doctors, they all knew who was the central personage of the cult. He was the hunter Itota, who, on the rare occasions when he appeared from the bush, resided in the village at the end of the vicinage, on the edge of the wilds. Vic was the one who spoke with him most. He was old and white-haired and upright, with the long, lined face of some ancient sea king. He had only one eye, and when he spoke his voice rolled like gravel. He had been through many stages of initiation in his time. His gun was older than he, a flintlock with a long slender barrel and shapely stock. The date 1863 could be seen very dimly on the brass sideplate. The gun had been used in the American Civil War, and had then been shipped overseas for sale to Itota's ancestors. Once it had backfired—right into Itota's eye, blinding it. A blacksmith had repaired the gun, nature had eased Itota's pain, and again he had killed many animals. The stock was thick with trophies. The first was the tail of a sable antelope, the noblest game in the forest, whose horns describe a half-circle two feet across. The soft sweeping hair of the tail on the stock was like a caress; underneath it you could see rows of brass studs on the well-rubbed wood, one for each kill. Itota could tell you about each battle. He knew the berries that antelope loved, he knew their habit of seeking the wet plains in the dry season, and which leaves of the forest they chose in the spring. When Itota succeeded in felling his quarry, when it staggered, its back sank as if to rest, and its eyes glazed over, he would turn to an anthill whistling praise for his hunter demon, now turned guide; then he would crouch down to the ear of the animal and pray for the soul within it.

In his actions were an ancient freedom and dignity worn into him during his continual roaming in the bush, where at every step he had to make his own judgments about the game. His personality was like some tree surmounting an anthill, looking out forever, the only living thing in the forest that rose high enough to survey the forest itself.

Itota had always been in Chihamba; it was generally supposed that he would be present in the ritual at its central moments, at the time of the Deep Voice. Could he be called an actor who could lose himself in a part? It was not that: in the ritual an actual identification flashed into being, for Itota was a shaman. No one, not even he, knew how far his powers extended. Once the ritual began there was a power afoot that devoured everybody, that would take over the white-haired old man and narrow him into the lightning flash. Afterwards his spirit would remain sunk in the earth for a time. Through the same power the earth would give birth to him again, finally delivering him out to all the village. And then, back home, he was just Itota, bee man, wax collector, always away on the hunt.

Throughout the villages the cult revived quickly, its message: "Never despair." A number of people had been initiated at a Chihamba fifteen years earlier, and those members would become doctors in this ritual. Such an adept was a priest as much as a doctor, for the ritual acted not only to heal the sick but to draw the community back into communion with its deity. The ritual the god desired was a four-day-long strategem that combined an initiation, a healing rite, a sacrifice, a revelation, and a rebirth.

Nyamuvwila and Engeniya had not entered the cult before, and would undergo primary initiation. Poor Nyamuvwila, married into a welter of haughty Kajima long-faces! They quarreled incessantly over her head, they meddled in the affairs of her children, mocking the misfortune of her daughter Engeniya. Nyamuvwila had practically been driven into leprosy by them all. But the god was going to open her way to bliss, if only for a moment.

Some who entered the cult were not sick or in trouble of any sort, but were drawn toward something in the bush that attracted them. The word "grandfather" was central to the discussions of the elders, even though no tongue dare pronounce his actual name. No one presumed to claim him as her own ancestor, for he belonged to everybody, like the rain. He rumbled and brooded down in the woods, splitting the darkness with his power hand, spilling out energies untold, producing cassava in plenty, and bestowing on his people the benefit of health. His passion would crack open the cold womb for the swarming sperm. He was an utterly beloved, if fearsome, grandfather, stumping around in their lives with an angry fist for the terrified shrimps of grandsons, but he was present with the people. I thought of the elders of my family; they were all gone.

As the time came closer, the men talked incessantly of the approaching ritual, and Vic returned from their confabulations with notebooks filled.

"It's the biggest ritual of all," he announced. "That name 'Shit ritual' is quite an irony. And it's old, no one knows how old. I've a hunch this is going to tell us more than all the other religions about the mysteries behind life—never mind that stuff about Africa being primitive; there are no primitives. This culture is infinitely complex, just as any culture is."

"All this just to help Nyamuvwila, Vic?"

"Yes. You see, here religion works by means of the social process. It's for people. Just watch."

Our own preparations began. I ordered from town dozens of rolls of film and fresh supplies of pencils. Vic broke the rules of his funding institute and claimed travel expenses that weren't travel expenses. They were actually gifts for informants. The travel fund had plenty left in it because our truck was out of order, while the informants fund was long since spent. The money came through and was distributed. In the kitchens women were brewing beer, a sure sign of religious fervor, and they obviously were enjoying themselves. This spectacle contrasted strongly with the previous state of misery and backbiting into which both the village and our family had fallen.

Samutamba paid Vic a special visit, anxious to impress upon him that the ritual centered on Samutamba Farm.

"You know what it's for, Mister Vic? It's to cure my wife; it's all put on for Engeniya." Vic wrote it down in his notebook.

"And who's going to be principal doctor, Samutamba?"

"Why, I am." He drew himself up; he was wearing his road captain's fez and military shirt, and the old frown of power and sorcery was in his eye. He bustled out into the rain to take control. Vic and I followed at a discreet distance and found a noisy group of doctors gesticulating in front of Nyamuvwila's hut.

Samutamba's voice had a cantankerous edge. It appeared that he intended to run Chihamba like a Shaking ceremony.

"But Samutamba, there's the chasing, the Voice, and . . ."

"It's a night ceremony, ninnies." He was so angry that he showed his filed teeth. "The patient has to shake. Now you people," his arm sawed up and down, "you're not going to drag in that old crap about the Grandfather, are you?"

Headman Lambakasa, a neighbor of Itota's, pushed to the front, his face glittering with serious intent. "The diviner gave us the words. 'Seek the Grandfather,' he said. And he is found with Chihamba. That cannot be modern, don't you understand? It is given us from long ago. Look, my friend, we are making this drum ritual for Engeniya and her mother, Nyamuvwila; leave it to those that remember it. Maybe you're a member, but you missed the last time when the spirit came; you were in town."

Samutamba's brow lowered. "Engeniya's my wife, not yours. I ought to know what's best for her."

Samutamba preferred the Shaking ritual for Engeniya, for by its means a woman could become an important doctor, especially if she were childless like Kandaleya, the eldest daughter of Manyosa. He tried to avoid the true Shit ritual, which demeaned a person and then blessed, whose principal medicine bore the meaning "the revelation of secret things." Samutamba didn't want too many secrets revealed. He was an individualist and liked to plan his own life.

"Samutamba." Lambakasa's voice was low. "Come over here a moment. Now we all know what the trouble is. Come to Chihamba with us. You don't believe Chihamba can help you, do you? Strange things can happen, for Grandfather has many powers. How can you be expected to remember him? You were only a small boy when you were caught by him the first time."

Truth was written all over Lambakasa's shining black face. Samutamba felt his shoulders relax, and a longing for the wild bush came over him, a memory of the days before the road-making. He gazed at the trees. A force seemed to draw him into the bush, seducing his will.

"I'll come," he said. "But I'm going to be head doctor."

Lambakasa sighed.

Back in the group of elders the arguments were resumed, but were eventually resolved in a convenient compromise. Samutamba would be doctor in charge of patients, Lambakasa was to be master of ceremonies, while the role of doctor of medicines was given to pinchy-faced learned Nyaluwema, the first wife of Sakazao. Itota was not seen at these gatherings.

Now the rain began in earnest. Lambakasa stood in front of Nyamuvwila's hut. "Bring the patients here," he called, and directed Nyamuvwila to take first place in front of the hut. She did so humbly.

"Come on, Engeniya, you're next."

"Hurry up, hurry up, Engeniya," said Samutamba officiously. He already had a medicine broom with which he proceeded to whisk his wife. She endured it patiently, but shot him a glance as if to say she knew who should be whisking whom. Behind her was gathering a long line of candidates. I recognized Yana, Masondi, Sani, Diana with Rene, Monica, Manyosa's son, Jerry, with women, men, and children from the villages around. I went to stand among them, and was immediately included in their growing comradely feeling.

A hand was on my shoulder; I looked around and saw Manyosa smiling at the thoughtful expression on my face. "What's this? You're a patient, are you, Mishy?"

"Yes." I had a reason. "Are you one, too?"

"No, no. I entered the cult a long time ago. I'm in an advanced grade now. But you and I can be friends of the bosom, mabwambu, as people are in Chihamba."

"Sure." I started to give her an enthusiastic handshake.

"Wait a minute. Don't do that. I'll teach you the special handshake for Chihamba. You must remember to put the force, ngovu, into it." She seized my hand and pulled. "Pull back," she told me. There was quite a tussle for a moment. "That's right. It gives strength to Chihamba." We did it once more, smiling.

Meanwhile, Nyaluwema took charge of the medicines and rattles. Each patient was to have a rattle of her own, which entailed much whittling and fitting. Nyaluwema came to our door with a cane mat protecting her head from the pouring rain. She brought the rich smell of wet cane in with her. When she had maneuvered through the door and put the mat down she brought something out from beneath it. It was a great resounding rattle, consisting of three round bronze-colored gourds mounted one on top of the other upon a baton, which penetrated each gourd through the center. The portion of the baton below the gourds swelled out into a bulb, handsomely carved, while the lowest end became a smooth handle. Each gourd was perforated with decorative holes. I turned the rattle upside down and observed a hollow carved in the butt end of the handle. Interesting. I restored it to its upright position, glimpsing yellow corn grains inside the gourds. The sussuration they made at every movement was exciting.

"This is your own rattle, Mishy," said Nyaluwema. I shook it with pride. Nyaluwema showed me the rhythm, and the right way to pass it from hand to hand. The action was similar to the handshake: you hold it out to your partner, who grasps it around the carved swelling with her hand above yours. Your partner pulls at the rattle as if to free it, but you tug back as if unwilling to relinquish it, thereby sounding the gourds. Only then do you pass the rattle over; you have given power to the rattle.

Nyaluwema warned me to look after the rattle well and to "put it away on the high shelf of your millet loft." Later, when the fieldwork was through and we arrived home, I came across the rattle in our baggage. "My rattle," and I remembered Nyaluwema's injunction. I tried it on the top shelf of a display cabinet. It seemed too real to be among our ornaments, so I put it on the kitchen mantel shelf, in the middle.

In the afternoon, when the rainstorm was over, the doctors assembled and quietly moved into the bush among trilling cicadas and dripping leaves. They were hunting medicines to fill Nyaluwema's winnowing basket, her basket of revelation. Lambakasa led the way, singing a plaintive song, and the others replied with the shush-she-shush, shush-she-shush of the new rattles. We followed behind. The medicines were for the patients, but they meant more than Western medication. Plant materials were selected from all over the bush, much as an artist chooses colors from a palette. In one sense, the medicines all together formed a picture, but the result was not a painting, and the aim was not the creation of a work of art. It reminded me of the symbolism found in a cathedral with many statues, each with a meaning that reinforces the meaning of the others, striking emotional echoes across and across the aisle. This seemed closer to the mark. Or was the basket of medicines like an Indian sand painting, being intended as a diagram of an idea? Using a kind of hieroglyphic language, it communicated complex religious statements that could not be formulated in words. Nyaluwema placed her pieces in the basket, twig over twig, root chip near root chip, bark shouldering bark. Each was a substance of power, and their interactions meant more than their individual meanings.

The doctors gave great honor to the first medicine, the Early Morning Tree. They crouched at the foot of the tree and prayed before striking the ground with hoes in search of its roots; these were pure white, symbolizing innocence, goodness, and wholeness. Then they took a twig from the Tree of Little Thorns. This meant affliction, the catching hold of a person. Then, wandering far, they came upon the most important tree for the Grandfather, the Tree of Revelation, musoli. Beneath this tree, which bears yellow pears, is seen the antelope, rare, vanishing, and heart-catching. The next medicine was the stone from the sugar apricot, the Nut of Time. The stone is exceedingly hard, like a chip of rock, never changing. Then came a leaf from the Swarm Tree, which means large crowds and processions. Swarms of bees are attracted to the countless flowers that come in the spring. Lastly, the Overnight Plant, which like the mole leaps out of the ground overnight, was chosen because it represented the rapid ousting of disease.

This collection was assembled much as a sentence is put together from different parts of speech, each "word" a complex symbol in itself. It was like a chant or prayer:

> I come, all white
> From my inmost root
> Up to the sunlight
> Candid and whole and good.

Spirit, your thorns
Catch and afflict us as we pass.
We ask you to catch us, healer,
You will help us to be free.

Journey into the deepest wilds
Seeking the pear tree that reveals.
Ready to turn—there is the tree—
The antelope, feeding, blest.

Caramel apricot
That ripens in the rains,
Its stone will not decay,
Alive to eternity.

God as sweet as nectar,
Sweeter than flowers of the berry tree
We are drawn to you—humankind—
Swarming like the bee.

The mole within the earth
Is the sickness beneath the skin.
At the spirit's touch, suddenly
It erupts and is gone.

By the time the doctors returned to the village the sky had
darkened with another storm. They took shelter under Nyamuvwila's kitchen roof and started preparing the medicines.
They lit fires and set little black pots to boil, adding pounded
leaves to the boiling water. It was a dark scene, with dark bodies
in rags manipulating a complicated art. The patients were
brought close, stripped to the waist, seated in a line, then each
received a sprinkling of the mixture. Catching sight of their
backs in the firelight I could see the speckles of pounded medicine on the glittering wet skin. The doctors mixed drinking
medicine, and also a powder containing rock salt and some of
the white root. Nyaluwema brought the powder around to our
hut that evening. She asked for our big rattle, then placed some
of the salt medicine on the hollow butt of it, and offered it to Vic

and me. We ate the mixture seriously, without using our hands, like babies, like Guinea Fowl before her dance and Manyosa at her European Dinner. Nyaluwema warned us with a twisted grin that we must not make love throughout the ritual if we wanted to be initiated as members. I pulled a face. Musona, listening from the side, was overcome with laughter and slapped his thigh in disrespectful delight, his legs curvetting around like an antelope's, long and slender. He was neither doctor nor patient.

That night the entire ritual community gathered around the fire. The patients were lined up and hustled to the door of Nyamuvwila's hut; she and her comrades were thrust in and the door was shut, leaving them in pitch darkness. The moment had come.

"Hehh!" barked a deafening voice, and they all jumped. Rattling thunder broke out from above, close to their ears. The sense of a power nearby haloed Nyamuvwila's skin. Everyone rushed hither and thither.

"He's come, he's come." "Who?" "Where?" Nyamuvwila blocked her ears and hunched her shoulders; she was being battered by bodies.

A single deafening crash—a thunderbolt! Someone leapt down on the crowd. Nyamuvwila's head collided with Yana's, and there was a flash. Was that lightning?

"Pus balls! Babyshitters!" burst out a deep voice in Nyamuvwila's ear. She felt her belly go loose. "This drum is for the babyshitters."

His voice began to roll like gravel. "What are you doing here, babies? *Come to me and let me break you apart.*"

Nyamuvwila made for the wall and stayed there, feeling her scalp come up with a tingle that gradually spread all over her head and neck until her skin was in a kind of glory.

That body was very close by, hot, smelling of overripe mushrooms and pear blossom. The ground shook a little. The companions were wailing, "Don't hurt us, dear Grandfather."

Nyamuvwila said in an abject voice, "Sir, I have come to ask you . . . to help . . . to cure . . ."

"Cunts!" he thundered uncompromisingly. Nyamuvwila jerked again, tears starting from her eyes.

Then, deeper than ever: "Bring me some food if you want to be cured."

"Er, yes, Grandfather." Nyamuvwila rummaged among her cooking pots. "I have a dish of love beans for you, Grandfather, red ones."

He ate, grunting.

"Aaah." There was a smacking of lips. "Now, what's that you said? Cures?" The vibration was still in the air, like distant thunder.

"Sir," someone said, "Nyamuvwila here has leprosy, sir. P-please won't you help her?" Nyamuvwila could not speak, she was weeping.

"H'm now. You'll see, old mother, you'll be cured. Come over here. I rename you Initiated One. You are going to cure yourself." Nyamuvwila at once was quiet.

Now Engeniya with trembling voice described her plight.

"Listen, lady, it will be a long time ahead, through many troubles, but eventually you will bear children. Meanwhile I name you Lady of Peace."

Yana came forward. "Such pain, at menstruation . . ."

"Woman, don't fret: the blood should flow. Now you are going to relish it. Your new name is The Satisfied."

And then Masondi . . .

They were through. There came a thunderous rattling, a hoarse laugh, and all was still.

Immediately the door was opened and they were hustled out. When Nyamuvwila reached the open air she turned back to peer into the darkness, but she could see nothing.

As for me, I was wishing on one side for more children one day. Didn't I have enough as it was? But there's no reasoning with a headstrong person like me.

Vic and I slept in separate beds that night, thoughtful and wondering.

Early next morning Nyaluwema came to our hut door with a rhythmic rattling. "Cho-kokoko-o choko-o!" she cried. It was the sound of a cock's crow. As we put out our heads, Nyaluwema scattered red cock's feathers all over us. "Hey, steady, Nyaluwema," we spluttered, picking feathers out of the corners of our mouths.

"Wake up. The Great Ordeal is beginning."

We followed her out to Nyamuvwila's hut, just in time to see Lambakasa hopping with an arrow between his toes toward the hut. When he reached it the others helped him rear up his foot and insert the arrow into the thatch. The arrow was the spirit itself, choosing out Nyamuvwila, and for this Lambakasa's hands, even with force, did not have power enough; it had to be his foot.

I was led into the woods, where the group of patients was collecting. The forest was alive with movement and the shrieks of children. It appeared that the doctors were out catching additional patients.

Samawika, Freddy, and Bobby skipped down the trail leading to the Kakula.

"A doctor," warned Samawika, and they all scuttled into the bushes. They watched as an elder went by. Strange; he was advancing backwards through the forest dragging a red cock along the ground between his legs. After him followed a line of doctors.

Samawika fled from the spot, leading the boys around in a wide circle over the dead leaves of the forest floor.

"Let's see if we can get in close. They're up to something and I want to watch. There's a huge white spirit down there," said Samawika.

"What's it like?"

"It's like a big ball of lightning! It's a monster," Samawika's eyes rolled dramatically.

"I don't want to see it," said Freddy, his eyebrows going up in the middle.

"Sho, sho, sho-sho-o!" came a rasping shout. They'd been observed. A man came crashing through the bush.

"Aka-ah!" cried Samawika. The doctor had him by the hair and grabbed Bobby with his other hand. Samawika and Bobby were laughing so much that they were caught, but Freddy dodged the doctor and ran all the way back to our hut without stopping.

Meanwhile, the rest of the doctors lined up our group to the sound of rattles and harmonized singing, then turned each one around facing home and set us walking backward into the bush, away from home. What we were walking toward no one rightly knew. Suddenly, at an arbitrary signal, the doctors shouted and chased us back to the village and into Nyamuvwila's hut, where we stood panting and puzzled. Without a pause the doctors came at us and chased us into the bush again, where we once more performed our backward walk. That took us just a little further. And so it went, the whole cycle being repeated in the course of the day some twenty times. Little ranks and cohorts of patients would arrive in the village from time to time, usually in the pouring rain. We would trot in perfect step into Nyamuvwila's hut and stand against the wall with our arms up, like manacled prisoners. The door would be shut. While we were imprisoned the doctors kept up an incessant sussuration on their rattles. Then off we had to go again toward the forest.

It was a long day. We were bored, patient, delighted, giggling, and horrified by turns. Some of the older patients asked me to call in at my hut for oil of wintergreen to rub on their aching muscles and rheumatic legs. Furthermore, they had been singing so loud that they could hardly speak; the neck would strain but no sound would come out. I rubbed the throats with wintergreen too. Later in the afternoon the doctors brought out long poles with forks at the ends. Armed with these, they chased the victims with greater zest than ever. The woods echoed with alarmed cries and laughter, panicked rushes and shouts.

"Those are slave yokes," whispered Vic during a brief respite. "They're made of milk wood, specially for Chihamba." We watched as the doctors caught Spider, the government odd-job man, and put his head in the yoke. The others broke out trilling with delight because Spider had shown no respect for the people's celebration.

I sighed and went back into the line, ready for more. Running with the others to and fro I wondered, "Am I acting out the slave victim? The milk tree yoke—is all this a profound kind of loosening up, an experience we have to go through, like girl's initiation? Or is this chasing the ordeal that comes before healing?" And as we approached our goal, "Vic said it was like the race of the apostles to the place of resurrection."

I was becoming so accustomed to finding my place in the line of patients that toward the end the chasing didn't seem to matter. What mattered was that at every backward approach the group drew nearer to its goal. The wonder that was growing inside me was reflected in the eyes of my companions. No one spoke; we were restive, but the doctors made us sit down in our line, where I now felt at home, with Yana in front and Masondi behind. The child patients behaved badly, playing with each other or fiddling with sticks. The doctors corrected their posture, straightening out their legs and turning their hands up so that they rested open and humble on their knees.

The doctors announced—now that we could hardly think— that we were ready to be questioned. They bent over the humble line and asked: "Who is it you want to see, eh?" "Come on, tell us his name." "What is his name, eh?" "You see, you don't know it." No one seemed able to answer. The doctors stood with arms akimbo and looked at the hopeless crew.

We were walking backwards again when Nyamuvwila stopped at an obstruction behind her. We peeped around and saw a high jumble of twigs closing off our path. "The hedge of mystery, chipangu," whispered Nyamuvwila. "To hide the revelation."

I held my breath. I could see down the line the shoulders pant, though the heads were still; through the silence nothing could be heard but the dim rolling of thunder. Rain began to pour, and now the doctors came up behind us, fierce and relentless, and drove us back to the village. Then immediately they drove us out of it again to the hedge of mystery. Meanwhile, accompanied by a fascinated Vic, the principal doctors hurried up a side path into the bush, taking with them the drums. They went directly to the place of revelation beyond the hedge. The hour had come.

At the patients' path minor doctors went up and down the line stripping the passive bodies to the waist. They marshalled us in our familiar line, this time, to our delight, facing the hedge. Nyamuvwila was in front, her plump form turning cheerfully about, a smile on her face, changing her anxious upward look into one of forgetful happiness. I was sure she'd forgotten her leprosy. I myself had forgotten—what were those troubles? Uncertainty, self-deprecation? Engeniya came next, very beautiful with her sloping shoulders, delicate head, and swaying body. Then Yana, my neighbor and comrade in line, who had those women's troubles; and I followed, restlessly peering. Behind me was Masondi with her burn, somber yet beautiful. And so they all came, young men from the market, Manyosa's in-laws, old women and young girls from the villages in Itota's area, all the odd last-minute catches the doctors could lay hands on, including Spider, Samawika, and Bobby. Samutamba, who was supposed to be the patients' organizer, stood with Vic, straddling about. Manyosa, friendly but watchful, attended to my catechism.

I looked up at her, catching her eye. "You'll tell me the name, won't you, Manyosa?"

"Just wait, wait. It's good for you to sit and be patient. Now see if you can tell me the name." I dared not answer.

"You don't know it, do you?"

"When are we going to get there?" muttered Nyamuvwila, uncomfortably shifting her buttocks; I looked around and bit my thumb impatiently. Manyosa pounced on me.

"Put your hand down, keep still," she hissed. I rapidly reassumed the correct posture and lowered my eyes before my novice mistress.

Deep in the bush we waited, stopped by the hedge of mystery. Suddenly the hoarse voice we all knew was heard.

"What's this rabble doing here?"

"We've come to do our Shit ritual, Sir."

We prodded pleadingly at the hedge with our rattles. A rush from the doctors drove us back, along with a crack of thunder that echoed through the forest. We huddled together, then crept forward again, crouching. There was a gap! Beyond glimmered something white. It moved—there was a hubbub of grunting— and something swelled up from the ground, dazzling in its whiteness.

Lambakasa was by our side. "It is the Spirit, diyi mukishi." The drums thundered.

I knew we had reached the crossing point. The whiteness reared and started to shake; was it the back of some great subterranean animal emerging here? Engeniya's eyes were a marvel. It roared at us; we trembled and sang as the drums tore out sound. What was this thing? Had the mother and father of all the cassava roots given birth to a monster animal? Was the earth itself alive and rising? Was the spirit of the land tearing open the mud of the surface and showing its lambent white spine?

Everyone was jerking and trembling to the din of music. "Grandfather! God of our Prayer! Revelation! Father of Increase!" Underneath the chorus my mind was repeating steadily the name I had heard from Vic: "Kavula! Kavula!"

In the rising syncopation of his dance the ancient one seemed about to break loose and walk all over his grandchildren. The aggressive rhythm surged through us. I was muttering, "You're great, you're great."

Nyamuvwila, Engeniya, and each woman in turn went forward and, taking her naked breasts in her hands, milked them out rhythmically toward the Grandfather in the royal salute. We all felt our own breasts tingle fiercely and harden. I could see my nipples stand up and swell; and strangely, even from the childless Engeniya, a sweet shower sprayed toward Kavula.

Lambakasa put the rattle into the hand of Nyamuvwila.

"Strike!" he commanded. "You must kill your Grandfather."

She looked at him in fear and awe.

"Go on. Kill him."

She took the rattle by the handle and, with the butt down, struck hard on the white solid object before her; and so did we all, setting our teeth and giving mallet blows fit to crack a skull. Thereupon a huge convulsion shook the thing, and it stilled, its ribs gradually caving in. There was a silence.

Lambakasa's voice chanted: "You have killed the Spirit."

The fact sunk in right down the line, faces were amazed; all of us smiled—we smiled. This was the revelation; we had got it.

Was there a corpse underneath? "Lift up the cover, Nyamuvwila, and look," said Lambakasa.

The white surface now was seen as a covering for something else. Nyamuvwila raised one corner of it.

"Eh!" she exclaimed. "Blood!"

The patients crowded around. She raised the cover further. Underneath appeared what seemed to be a beheading block, dripping with fresh blood.

"The Grandfather, where is he?" asked Nyamuvwila. In her mind's eye she had expected to see a recumbent figure with teeth, wearing stripes of red, white, and black. But under the cover was nothing save a framework of sticks, the hard up-turned block of a mortar, and the blood. The shrine was empty.

"Your blow has made you innocent," declared Lambakasa. We looked at each other, puzzled, yet with understanding. To each patient Lambakasa gave the same assurance, and blessed each one of us on the head with a handful of cassava meal from inside the shrine. The white spirit was being transferred to us all. We had performed a sacrifice in fear and humility, and somehow we had been redeemed.

Everyone rose and formed a triumphal procession. Now we saw that it was evening, for the pale orange light was seen half around the earth, far between the trees. We set out walking on the long trail back to the village; everyone was smiling like a brother, like a mother, like a sweetheart. Didn't we hold hands? The narrow path was broad, somehow; everyone walked abreast, free. Manyosa and I became friends of the bosom there, Vic and Samutamba also, everyone paired off in friendship. All our heads were held high. It's a fact that I've never been so happy before or since. We were singing, "We are innocent, we are free." The company that walked back was that.

When we reached the village Lambakasa led us to the central fire. He picked up a firebrand and struck it on the ground. His arms and legs spread with the effort of realization, he shouted, "It's done!"

Quietly we rested in the village, drank a cup of millet beer, and went off to supper and bed.

Something very important had been completed, which I

somehow couldn't come to grips with. We lay awake in our separate beds for a long time talking.

"There are all sorts of puzzles in this . . . this performance," I said. "To begin with, why weren't we told his name?"

"It's not just an Ndembu problem, Edie. It's a universal one. They're trying to express what can't be thought of rationally. Artists, poets try to break into that domain, they try to express It by various strange means."

"It's the same It," I said. "But you never actually see It."

"No. It's like Yahweh. When you open the ark of the covenant it's empty. It's the same with the empty tomb after the resurrection. I know another case like that. It's Moby Dick. Remember 'the ungraspable phantom of life'? Ahab lifts his harpoon and strikes it."

And I said, "That point of destruction—the crossing place—I love that. We go up as far as we can to the spirit, with our symbolic contraptions; we use all those odd means, as you say. The spirit comes close and listens to this material fabric they've got ready for him; how can he resist it when it roars and grunts and twitches? He comes down and takes it over, coalesces with it."

"Yes," said Vic, "and they immediately sacrifice him. That's what he wants. He gives himself for human social regeneration. We can't grasp this."

"No. Engeniya was dumbfounded. I'm dumbfounded."

"Kavula is formless energy," said Vic, sitting up. "Like the lightning flash. Pure act. Why, it's like what Aquinas said. He isn't acted upon, but it's he that keeps everything going, the crops in the fields, people and their interactions . . ."

"Yet he's a person."

"Yes. It's strange how important that is. He's unpredictable. He threatens, frightens people. And then gives benefits. It's just the opposite of reason. It's . . . antistructure. You have to be loosened up to understand him."

"And the whiteness?"

"Ah, I'm going to write about that. Something to do with

absence. Absence . . . made visible . . ." There was the sound
of breathing, and Vic was asleep.

I had my hands behind my head, still thinking. Then I bent
over and pulled a book out of the shelf. What I was looking for
was in Rilke's Fourth Duino Elegy. Yes, you could put the Ger-
man something like this:

> When the mood is on me
> I wait below the puppet platform.
> No, it's not waiting, it's watching
> —A gaze so total that in the end,
> to humor and rock my baby-longing,
> Look, an angel breaks in to play.
> He can't resist trying out the puppet shells.
> Angel and puppet, now there's a spectacle!
> Then comes together
> What we, dragged along by the motion and swaying of time
> Keep tearing apart, simply because we exist.
> I see growing out like a rainbow
> From the years, from the vagaries of time,
> The circumference
> That encompasses our whole wandering confusion.
> And over us and across
> The angel is playing.

The next day each patient was to be given her own shrine. Lambakasa and the doctors congregated by our camp footpath, so
we joined their ranks. We all set off down the path on a new
route, which did not take us far from the village this time; we
were in search of a powerful bundle of branches for the shrine.
The bundle was called the kantonga, which meant "thought
bundle." As the doctors walked they sang and their rattles re-
sounded. Halfway down the path Lambakasa paused, examin-
ing the bush with his eyes. Then he plunged in among some
stately trees right behind our camp. He pointed out one particular tree as "the Greeting Tree," around which we gathered. It
was a tree with white roots, as in the previous set of medicines,

but of a different species. This one had a touch of the familiar, like all the medicines for the thought bundle. It was the Tree Cassava, sacred to Chihamba. The two great loves of the Ndembu, the immortal cassava and the forest, were united in this magnificent living form, the Ikamba da Chihamba tree. Below, the roots were immensely thick, white and flaky with starch, but inedible for humans.

Lambakasa crouched at the foot of the tree and spoke into its heartwood where the spirit lay. Before the bole he placed a pellet of white clay, the sign of communication with the spirits. The angle of his head showed that his heart was open and well-disposed toward the spirit—his liver was white.

"Come quickly, show yourself, medicine root," he commanded.

Suddenly Itota's wife pressed forward with a hoe, knowing something. Without hesitation she turned up the soil at a certain spot below the tree and at once encountered a root. A cry went up from the crowd of doctors. She bent down close to clear away the deep red humus around the root and expose it. Having done so, she lifted her hoe and struck a wound into its white body. Another cry went up, followed by mournful singing: "He is wounded, he is wounded."

Lambakasa bent down with a basin of oil. He compassionately dressed the wound with oil and touched it with the base of the rattle. A sigh of relief seemed to go up from the tree. Lambakasa took an ax and matter-of-factly chopped through the root at either end and loosened it. Then, using their rattles, the doctors carefully lifted the section onto the medicine basket. They had won their first medicine. Everyone smiled and clapped rhythmically; Nyaluwema blessed us all beside the eyes, marking us with white clay.

Now we collected a milk tree stem, a blood tree frond, a twig from the pear tree of revelation, then three that they bunched together to make a whisk broom. We had often seen doctors dip these brooms into medicine and slap them on the back of a patient. The names of the branches all implied the sweeping away of witchcraft creatures; even the rhythm of the names when spoken reminded one of slapping: "Mu*hotu-hotu*, mu*kombu-kombu*, *mutu-tambu-lolu*." These were added to the bundle for health. Nyaluwema added a cassava cutting from her garden and prepared a basket of red love beans and another of white corn seeds, also a white hen. All together her symbols composed a poem, evoking memories of great days after hunting, of taking one's ease by the log fire, the fragrance of cooking still in the air, the family reunited, the tall young lads hoping to catch a glimpse of the beautiful girl-cousin from the group that had broken off from the village some years back. Here were unity again and relief, suckling babies, fresh huts with a loaded kitchen loft, the sizzling of fermenting beer, sweet dreams with one's arm crooked under the head of the devilish handsome hunter, while his rested on the small of one's sensitive back. All this was in the thought bundle.

That morning Nyamuvwila's shrine was consecrated, and then Engeniya's. When Engeniya's was finished and the doctors had gone away, Samutamba squatted brooding by the little construction. The exuberantly leafy column of the thought bundle stared him in the face while he pondered.

In the afternoon Vic and I received a visit from Lambakasa, Nyaluwema, and their band of assistants, who brought a white hen. Nyaluwema was carrying her medicine basket and a new thought bundle. Vic and I looked at each other: was this for us?

Nyaluwema put down her burdens in the yard and proceeded to dig a good big hole, directly outside our dining hut doorway. She and the other doctors sang while they worked, accompanied by the rattles of the juniors. All of them acting together lifted the thought bundle and planted it in the hole, tamping it down with the butts of their rattles. Then they dug a little moat around it. They took the beans and corn and sowed them in a thick ring in the moat. Bending low, they spoke a blessing into the ring and covered the seeds over; they dug a small trench at the side facing our door. They turned to the medicine basket in which rested a section of root from the Tree Cassava, a piece as

broad as a man's thigh, damp, and white as chalk. They deli-
cately lifted this fragile cylinder and inserted it into the groove
they had left, an earthy setting for a white jewel. It lay beside
the moat of beans like a bridge, an exit from the thought bundle
to the world, and seemed to look out of the earth with an eye
of white, like the rising sun. We immediately loved it as it lay
securely settled, at home with us.

The doctors had a last task, to crown our small citadel. To do
this, Lambakasa bit into the neck of the white hen, a pious act
of sacrifice. He quickly held the bleeding neck over the column
of sacred branches so that the flowing blood could strengthen
the shrine. I had unconsciously gritted my teeth while I
watched, adding my own strength. Lambakasa impaled the
fowl's head on the highest branch of the shrine, leaving the
mouth gaping open. Lambakasa said: "Its spirit looks out, it
looks out." The shrine was now plugged into two poles, at the
top and the bottom, humming with power. Lambakasa then
sang and drew three white lines in clay from the foot of the
thought bundle, over the white bridge, and right to the door of
our dining hut. The shrine was complete.

That evening we ate the white chicken roasted for supper—
an ordinary dinner, and yet not ordinary.

The next day at noon, while flies were buzzing around the
impaled head, a "drrrrrrr" was heard in the village. It was a car.
It was the missionaries. It couldn't be; it was. Our family was
eating in the dining hut when we realized they were actually
approaching our hut. The missionaries obviously intended to
ring the doorbell—if they could find one—in order to hand in
a tract. I got off my stool and turned around. One of them was
the lady doctor at the local hospital fifty miles up the road, the
other was her assistant. I saw the two faces staring fascinated at
what had been planted between them and the door. A change
came over the faces, the decision to ignore what they saw, and
with controlled expressions the ladies slipped past the bloody
shrine, holding their dark blue linen dresses so that the spikes
of the sticks would not catch them.

"Do come in. How are you?" I said.

"Very well, thank you."

"Will you have some tea?"

"Oh, yes. Thank you." The ladies drank. There was a silence. Vic came over to me and murmured, "Now's our chance to help the Ndembu on the medical side. Shall we . . . ?" I nodded, and he went aside and rummaged in his pockets.

"How's the hospital doing these days, doctor?" I asked benevolently.

"Ah, I fear, very short of funds as usual. But we do our best. These Ndembu . . ."

"Yes, yes," I said somewhat impatiently. Vic was taking a long time searching his pocket; there was a hole in it, and money kept getting lost in the lining of the jacket. At last he found what he sought and, after considering it sadly for a moment—he was a Scotsman—presented the bundle of cash to the lady doctor. All the time the devilish shrine watched us through the door.

The visit proved to be brief.

"Er, I think it's time . . ." The thin one looked at her watch, then rose, with thanks on her lips. We all exchanged nervous smiles, and I showed them out.

"Ooh-ah!" The doctor recoiled involuntarily as she came into the open. As I watched I saw her acknowledge her enemy—the paganism against which she had fought all her life—with one glance of hate. Still, she had in her purse Victor Turner's donation to the mission hospital.

In a couple of weeks the thought shrine was alive with bean shoots, and a big hand-shaped frond projected from the top of the cassava cutting. It had taken root. The shrines of Nyamuvwila and Engeniya were doing well and were beginning to take effect. Nyamuvwila forgot her previous reaction to the idea of hospital and went to the leper sanitarium, where she was easily cured. Yana looked rested. She told me her period pains had entirely vanished. What was really strange was that when I came to change the dressing on Masondi's burn and lifted off the gauze, time seemed to have jumped. There was nothing but a healthy scar. Engeniya seemed happy enough to wait indefinitely; Samutamba was busy repairing road drains, so she had peace.

In Kajima people laughed at jokes again. Now was the time to wind up Chihamba and switch back to normal life. Everybody gathered in a close crowd at Nyamuvwila's shrine and received from Lambakasa a small pellet of cooked cassava. Vic and I watched Lambakasa's face, giggling a little.

"Yipu!" he said, and everyone flung her pellet into the shrine.

"Wohoo!" Laughter went up, because the pellets whitened the ground around the sacred twigs. Consisting as they did of the people's staple diet, domesticated and cooked, the pellets signified the means of subsistence, focused on the shrine in this one last act. It was now time for the Thunder Friends to bathe, cut their hair, put on their best clothes, and gather for a beer party. Chihamba was over.

Chihamba always cured. Even I in the course of time gave birth to a couple more babies. Often when I regarded the determined chin of the elder and stroked the wafting auburn hair of the youngest I recalled the savagery and power of Kavula.

"Babyshitters! Bring me my love beans and I shall heal you." In return we had killed him. The gravel voice of Itota rang in my mind, a man whom Vic understood better than I:

> I see in the lean black's ancient face
> The crimson empires through the forest creep
> Hoarse veins of proud and pounding war
> And for his desolation weep.
>
> I know no melody of yellow fruit
> Grafted with deft and modern hands
> So sweet as that unyielding wood
> That cenotaphs his buried lands.

Victor Turner

RETURN

OUR FIELDWORK WAS FINISHED. With a jolt we turned our thoughts back to England and became conscious of the whole world of concerns that used to bother us so much: politics, dissertation, and academic career. There were practicalities to attend to: I opened Freddy's arithmetic notebook, in which he was supposed to have been making regular progress while I was otherwise occupied, only to shut it again quickly. It was hopeless, the mess was frightful; he was in danger of being kept down a grade when he went back to school. I made a mental note to bully, drill, and bribe the child to improve, and then put the whole thing out of my head.

We arranged our affairs and packed. The villagers seemed to grow more demanding for a time, greedier. We told each other we were thankful we were going. In whatever way we behaved toward them, they insisted that we were betraying them by leaving: they would no longer have the benefit of medical help, or pay, or meat, or plenty of visitors. We ourselves hated packing, hated the feeling that we were only half there, semi-transparent, already gone overseas, at least in our interests. Yet it felt as if everybody I had ever loved was going to be left behind; we loved even the arguments, the disapproval we felt for them sometimes, their disapproval of our different ways; we loved the forthrightness of it. And when they came and stood by our truck now that it was full, with the two boys settled in their customary niches in the back, and the grass huts standing empty, and Musona doing his last bit of helping—and his last private business of selling our cast-off clothing to his relatives—we stood there stupid with the inevitability of having to leave. Of course I loved them all. Of course it was tactless of me to try to kiss Manyosa and Nyamuvwila goodbye; they didn't have the custom of kissing in public, but blew in the ear. They endured my kiss. They were going to let us disappear out of their lives quietly, the way Manyosa had left for Ndola—in the village one day and gone another. Musona told Vic: "Everyone feels that it is your death."

Then Itota came—not through the village, not down any known path, but from an unexpected direction through the bush. We saw once again the white head, the tall figure wavering and solitary, grand without realizing it, hurrying from behind the kitchen to say goodbye to Vic. He was there, solidly there, striding as he stood, shaking hands with Vic for the last time. Palm, thumb, palm, thumb. They spoke, but no one knew what they said.

For the last time I wondered who he was. Was he the earth-risen Chihamba spirit, just as they said?

We simply drove off down our familiar Mwinilunga road. Of course I was crying, and the children as usual laughed because I cried whenever I left a place. I shook my head clear of the tears and tried to think what lay ahead. We had to reach the copper town, Chingola, that night, three hundred fifty miles down the dirt road. The weather was awful: gray, with torrential rains dinning on the roof of the cab, pounding on the tarpaulin that the boys had drawn over themselves at the back, soaking the leathery flat leaves of the bush, and swirling the sand around the giant anthills as we passed. We thought uneasily of the rumors that had drifted in from the missionaries, that the road ahead was flooded and might be closed. My memory has healed over that long muddy nightmare of a road, as we went smack at a pool, creating giant fans of water; as we survived skidding escapes, slosh, slosh, smack again; and rain, rain, deafening on the cab all the time, until at last, with a kind of relief, we reached a particularly miserable stretch that someone had been trying to repair. There in front—we were already upon it—was a skimpy rank of logs laid in corrugation across the swamped road.

"Look!" shouted Vic above the din. He was pointing to a gully as we passed. We saw Transporti itself on its side, abandoned in the ditch. This was serious. Around the very next bend another big vehicle, a truck from Norton's store, lay tilted on its side. Our faces gazed out at them fascinated, while our own little pickup skittered by. I don't think the children and I realized the skill of the driver, for he kept the truck on the road until we reached deep water.

We were at the rim of a small plain, a natural meadow, which the rain had turned into a lake; the road went down into it and disappeared. A busy sight met our eyes. Two American boys were driving toward us in an open jeep across the deep water; how, I couldn't understand. They seemed to know where the road surface was underneath. They were coming back from towing over a car carrying missionaries, which we saw departing on the further shore. The two young fellows came riding back to us upright in the jeep, and landed. It was easy. Vic climbed out of the truck and discussed with them the feasibility of our truck making it through; then they all looked underneath at our tailpipe. I climbed out along with the children, who thought this was fun and danced about. I thought it was interesting, too, remembering my resourceful mother and her adventures in the Himalayas. After a moment the men decided that our tailpipe was on the low side, but that if Vic kept driving the exhaust gases pumping through the tail pipe would keep the water out. So we all clambered aboard, sitting hunched up with the effort to keep moving or else. Vic let out the clutch—it was like a duck or swimmer letting himself out from the riverside—and into the water we went. And he did go on, did go on, for thirty yards.

There came a jolt. Vic pulled at the wheel, gunned the engine, pulled the other way; there was something under the water, a rock perhaps. He roared the engine while the wheels milled around, then the engine stopped with a pathetic ploop. Pressing the starter was useless; the truck had died.

Rene let out a little wail. The boys danced all the more on top of the baggage behind. I fondled Rene and looked about me. The water was in the cab and was lapping around the typewriter under my seat. I stayed bending, my hand wet. "The typewriter's shot, Vic," I said.

"You stay there," he said, and took off his shoes and socks and rolled up his pants. We looked back at the shore. Toward us came the two American boys, walking into the water in their beautiful white socks, which they didn't think of taking off. How glorious they looked in their fresh safari gear! They strolled deep into the water, slouched toward us casually, grinned, and fastened their rope onto our axle. Then they returned to shore with their rope, turned the jeep to face the way we had come, made the rope fast to the back of their jeep, and drove toward the Ndembu for thirty yards until we had been dragged high and dry. It was easy. After that they towed us right across the lake as if it were a cruise, to the Chingola side, and there they accepted my goggling gratitude. I hadn't stirred from my seat and footbath.

The truck stood motionless on the Chingola road while its sides ran with rivulets of water. After a while we tried the engine, and it started. Now we hurried on to make up for the delay. There was no traffic on the road at all; we had seen all there was. Now the bush was cleared here and there, now appeared a few Kimberley brick huts, then actual gardens. Now Vic pointed out a Coca-Cola sign tacked against a hut, which bore the word "Tearoom." Now we saw a house with windows. Windows! Then more of them.

Rene gaped, "What's that?" She pointed to the left, where an unfamiliar pillar projected up from one of the houses.

"A chimney," we told her; she looked blank. In a trice we were on a blacktop road, and there to our numbed sight appeared the vast chimneys and derricks of the copper mine, a city of machinery. Our heads swiveled this way and that. Chingola looked as big as London, not a mere township of seven thousand people with one mine, one movie theater, and one shopping street. We drove right into the metropolis and stopped with unerring instinct outside the town bar (for men only). A fresh item of news was on everyone's lips: the last car before the road closed had just made it through. We looked about, interested; which car was that? Why, it was us, of course.

Vic went into the bar. He came out and spoke to me.

"Apparently it's a great occasion," he said. "Just for once they'll let you in and we'll celebrate."

We went in, children and all, in our unspeakably old clothes, smiling as if we were crazy. The miners supporting the bar turned. They never spoke, but I gather we made quite a sensation. Afterwards, we staggered out to look for lodgings, and again, ragged as we were, they took us in at Brown's Hotel.

We didn't realize how changed we were. Every practical task seemed ridiculously easy after living hand–to–mouth in the bush. The next day we shopped for clothes, and by that action started growing into the different life. If we had not been fully laden—indeed, pregnant with field material—we might have been alternately nostalgic and savage about the inequities between town and the bush. But we were holding our breaths, as it were, in case we burst. We knew we would have to set out the Ndembu social structure, set it out so that readers could see it in the process of working. All sorts of social tricks used by the Ndembu had been docketed away in our minds and notebooks, ready to be analyzed—how people used each other within the arrangement of their society, what happened in a social crisis, and so on. The tremendous symphony of the religion kept playing its themes deep in our minds. We were going home still imagining ourselves to be dialectic materialists, but the contact with religion had been made and the damage to our dogmas had been done. The theoretical "baby," when it arrived, was very different from the one in Vic's original grant proposal.

Our personal philosophy had gone like this: Bad times and good times, these we have all had. We are supposed to suffer the bad times as decently as we can. In the good times we should go ahead and teach the children world literature and classical music, and even become peacemakers in times of departmental factionalism, and go-betweens for marrying couples.

But why? Because our good parents expected us to be decent helpful people, and their parents expected it of them, and so on back to the apes? These Ndembu performances we had seen, of deep color and emotion, were they just a game? Even in the games we knew, such as soccer, the best players put their all into their struggles. The roar of the forces of production was quiet compared to the urgent howl of those crowds. And classical music, full of devotion, beckoning and calling toward something, often in the shamanistic mode, what of that? The radical idealist's "good life for all" was not found in the starving composer's garret or Rembrandt's unworldly system of priorities. Our job was to go home and analyze a primitive religion, a system we had found so complex that the word "primitive" became a lie. Concerning the curious matter of the killing of a figure called Kavula, and the great happiness resulting from it, all psychological and sociological explanations were bound to fail; because we and the Ndembu knew it was more than that, just as the mystic in her humility knows more than the theologian.

Suffice it to say, we did drop our "explanatory materialism," mainly because it did not seem the right tool to use, the right lens with which to take the picture, the right measuring rod to apply; in other words, the right method.

When Vic and I were reestablished in England we were heartsick for Africa; never mind the handy gas range, the flush toilets of civilization, we had lost our own family. All that we could do now was work. Then, a year later, with Vic's dissertation written, and the children back at school after a bout of chickenpox, there came a night of certainty and meaning. It so happened that when I went to bed—unreasonably mournful at the end of a long period of effort—my sleep settled and settled until all the strain, all the useless material, were drained away before the morning. Suddenly the valves of my mind were opened and I had a dream. I was back in Kajima. My heart turned over, it dissolved like a thundercloud at the sight of the overgrown track and the plaza that opened out as I moved toward the chota. There were people there—Manyosa. Manyosa did not look at me; everything was taken for granted. Nyamuvwila was there, passing on one side, Mangaleshi too; she fell behind as I walked on. I put out a hand to greet someone; no hand touched mine, but everyone was present, their faces relaxed. My heart expanded with happiness; I was actually back, I was actually back. Joy and certainty spread until my range of sight opened out to the entire village. I seemed to widen and glide into the whole of it, I was it, lifted from touch and tread. I was home.

POSTSCRIPT

MANY YEARS PASSED, and eventually the day came when I could go back in the flesh to this village that I knew so well. Real years have changed Kajima. All the houses are of mud brick now, and there are fewer of them in any one village. At the same time the population has tripled, resulting in severe deforestation all around Kajima, right over to the Kakula River and beyond. The people are hungry and buy subsidized food from the missionaries, food that originates in South Africa. It is not commonly known that South Africa is busy throwing economic chains over the new independent southern African states.

Musona is still there in Kajima. He is headman now, just as Vic predicted. He is wrinkled, of course, and his Nyachintanga face is cavernous, but I discovered that his legs still curvet like an antelope's when he laughs—if a little shakily. Wasn't I old, too, needing glasses at every turn? Musona is disappointed that he did not appear under his own name in Vic's books. He has joined the Christian Fellowship, a Pentecostal breakaway from the Plymouth Brethren, has developed into a kindly personality, and has become an honored elder and village judge.

Old Master Kajima died and was buried upright in his grave, as befits a hunter. Manyosa is but a memory; they have grown used to her death now, just as I have become accustomed to

Vic's. So, Manyosa, that was my last farewell. Didn't we both know it, my friend? I wish I could have met again many of the old ones: Nyamuvwila; wafwa dehi—she's dead—they told me. Chikasa, wafwa dehi; She-Jackal, wafwa dehi; Chautongi, wafwa dehi (she's practically a Christian saint now); Mbimbi, wafwa dehi; Muchona, wafwa dehi; Nyaluhana, wafwa dehi; Lambakasa, wafwa dehi; Itota, wafwa dehi; Mwenda died of malaria soon after her initiation; and at last the great Samutamba died, but more of that will follow.

Who could have guessed that I should meet alive and well, now a very pleasant person, none other than Evita, Evita the hooker. She joined the B'hais, a new liberal religion, and her voice has toned down several decibels. You can look into her face without pain now, and share a decent cup of tea. As the old Grandfather said, never despair of anybody. Then Nyachitela, my buddy the witch, is apparently no older, and a lot warmer-hearted. She's just as perky, and is a helpful assistant at curing ceremonies, which was not the case previously. About curing ceremonies, that I'm keeping under wraps.

Let me go on teasing my readers a little longer. They will know what happened to Vic three years ago; he went to join his old friend Samutamba and there they are drinking kachai out of a teapot in some grass hut in no heaven or other place imagined in the great religions. And I am left, still trying to be an advocate for the Ndembu in my own way.

Stories assailed me from all sides in the new Kajima. Imagine me summoned out of my house to greet a visitor: we shake and clap hands. He's broad–shouldered, a young man in his prime, handsome and educated. I look at him curiously. He's well dressed too, with a mustache and polished shoes. He speaks to me in excellent English, and I become even more polite. He introduces himself as Elias Clifford Sakuwaha of the Zambian Air Force. I'm quite mystified. What is he doing here? "Don't you remember me?" he asks, and lifts up the cuff of his well-pressed pants at the ankle, and pulls down his sock. On the brown skin I see a scar. Ye–es, don't I remember a sore on an ankle? And I look into his face, foolishly seeking a narrow gnome-like visage. But isn't there something about the curve of the brow, wasn't that Yana's curve? He smiles; it can't be. "Nyakumesa!" I exclaim. "Is it really you?"

Now this is quite impossible, but quickly he starts to speak, partly laughing, partly full of the impulse of storytelling. "I was frightened of you," he says. "I had to come every day, every day, and it hurt."

"I know." Tears in my eyes.

"You, a white lady, what would you do to me . . . ?"

"I knew you felt like that; I know exactly" (a little kid of four).

"I remember how the pus poured out, the pain when you removed the bandages. And I had a wobbling walk; they called me Mwendu Nswadyi, 'Garbage-leg'."

"I worried about you, Nyakumesa; I couldn't sleep at night. I wondered if you were going to make it. And then, later, you know, we very much liked your coming around every night for milk."

Seeing him was like a miracle performed before my eyes: that such a swollen-bellied undersized runt, narrow-faced, starved, and crippled, should now be perfectly well and, in fact, beautiful. Just his speaking English so easily struck me as wonderful, and his power of self-expression, his ego-consciousness, his own memory: "I shall never forget coming every day for dressings"—his eyes gleamed—"and getting nice things to eat, bread, sweets . . ."

Nyakumesa had transformed the milk and dried meat into something delectable over the course of time. The course of time: this is what Nyakamesa and I have been borne in; regarded like this we seem to have been passive, this miracle has just happened, and all those years were nothing.

Nyakumesa was now telling me about the interim, how his father was determined to send him to school, how in that re-

remote village his father had become a bee man, made beehives, and sold honey and honey beer to support Nyakumesa at school. Nyakumesa remembers Kandemba, his little pal, of course. Kandemba is now known as Ted Ndeleki, prison warder (retired), and is at present a farmer. Dumb Dora is married, with a family. And Samawika, Bobby's pal at the Thunder rites, is now known as Mr. Stanley G. Sakuwaha, professor of political science at Chalimbana Training College at the capital.

"Political science! That has to be Marxist political science, from my knowledge of Zambia." So the wheel turns. . . .

And now, you ask, what happened to Samutamba? I had a photograph of Samutamba with me in New Kajima, showing him in his genial mood. He was wearing his road captain's fez, with his face bisected by that long Humphrey Bogart smile. I showed this picture around a group of friends. Mangaleshi saw it and, to my surprise, gave a gasp of pleasure, then looked sideways, remembering. What was she thinking?

"He died in 1972," was all she would say. One day, later, an oldish woman came to look at the photographs, again amid a group of excited viewers. "I'm Engeniya," she told me, giving that free challenging look of hers from among those bewildering wrinkles. She gazed at the photograph of Samutamba, but never commented on it. It was her elder sister Teresa who told me the story. The final drama started when Kandaleya, the elder daughter of Manyosa and former teacher of my daughter Rene, was stricken down. She could not use her legs and body, and died soon afterwards. Samutamba had killed her. It was he, of course, who had made her barren all those years; now he was finishing his dire work. The village rose in fury. Samutamba had always drunk too much, he was always violent and terrible, a bitter addict, and a worse enemy than ever now that the old master had died and Samutamba's rival Musona had succeeded him. They rose and drove him out of his brick house, tore his family from him, and sent him off to take refuge several miles up the road. Musona showed me the stretch of wasteland where his house had been, now just a level weedy patch.

Teresa continued the story sadly. "He had two sons, and one of them was only two months old. He never saw his newborn son again."

But then he had fathered sons at last! Had the new clinic beside the Kajima road been issuing him tetracycline for his gonorrhea? Engeniya said no. I wondered if Engeniya had taken other measures to have children, or had Samutamba simply recovered, as Kavula had predicted? Whatever the case, it was too late to alter his personality. No one could stand him in his new quarters and he was forced to go further afield, to the traditional chief's village. The chief was a drinking man like himself, but nevertheless the people drove him out again. The next news that came through was from Kabwe, the ex-colonial mining town of Broken Hill. Samutamba had reached the town deadly sick. Mangaleshi explained it was something to do with his legs and body. "At Kabwe Hospital they refused to admit him because he did not have the money for his body to be buried in their graveyard. So he went out and wandered up the road, where he fell dead"—my old friend dead in the dirt. "Someone saw the body and threw it into the river."

Mangaleshi shuddered at her own words. I looked down and closed my eyes. "I'm sorry."

A month after this disclosure a young boy was brought to me with a one–and–a–half–inch triangular rent in his shin, an injury sustained when falling off a bicycle. He was a serious lad of fourteen, with a long heavy face, rather ugly. We sent out in two directions to find the drunken clinician, but he was in none of the usual places. I looked in my medicine box. There were surgical needles, there was anesthetic and a hypodermic syringe, and there were quantities of antibiotic cream. So there was no getting out of it. With the help of Musona's grandson Jerry and my assistant Bill we set up my bed as an operating table, and tried to see what Samutamba's son could stand. Yes, it was Chinyama, the elder of the two. The boy stood up to the ordeal well; after all, we were merely a trio of amateurs. I had to give little injections of painkiller around the site first, then ask the boy if he felt anything.

"Nothing."

Then I had to wash myself carefully, cleanse the ragged wound, put on antibiotic cream, then get the needle down inside the mess to lace together the inside flesh—Samutamba's flesh and blood. Having tied those threads up and trimmed them short, I had to dig with the needle into the black outside skin—how strong it was—and draw together the tear itself, just like mending a coat. I was out of breath with the effort. Chinyama needed one or two more shots before we were through. We slopped on plenty of healing cream and closed the whole thing up with sticking plaster. Chinyama jumped off the bed and ran off to play. "Come back! Take these pills," I called, and gave him some tetracycline.

The boy's younger brother, a round-faced lad, had been named by Samutamba "Kajima"; the spirit of the old man must have come to Samutamba in a dream. Both children were doing well at school, but Chinyama was given to melancholy. When I changed his dressing next day I told him the story of Samutamba, Vic, and the teapot of millet beer. "Your father was Vic's best friend," I said. And then I saw in the child's face what I had never hoped to see again—Humphrey Bogart's heart-catching smile.

INDEX